GENDER AND FINANCE

This book examines the world of finance and the role of gender within it. It looks at the financial services industry, arguably the most powerful and remunerative sector that exists, and shows how it was created by men for men.

The author explains how historically women were excluded, how minimal progress has been made, and outlines how the sector still needs to change to function effectively in a modern, equal opportunities world. Addressing gender inequality in financial services is of utmost urgency and importance because of the extent to which it affects women in all stages of life. Women's exclusion in financial services is also mirrored by how men have been excluded from parenting through a similar set of societal expectations, government legislation and corporate policies. The author maintains that to succeed, we need to address both financial services and parenting. To do so we need regulatory support. Because of its power and dominance, the financial services industry has the opportunity to lead this change and to champion gender equal practices. These practices are economically beneficial to all participants, not only female employees and consumers. We all need these benefits as we rebuild our economies following the COVID-19 pandemic. The book makes an important contribution to the critical and increasing awareness of gender concerns. It presents insights drawn from original research and data about gender biases.

The book is an essential secondary text for a range of university courses, including economics, finance and accounting, business studies and gender related courses, as well as MBAs and Executive Education programmes that focus on gender in business. It is also a must read for policy makers, managers in financial services institutions and any other businesses that seek to attract the growing market of female consumers, employees and business leaders.

Dr. Ylva Baeckström is a researcher in finance at King's College London and an experienced banker, entrepreneur and psychotherapist.

Contemporary Issues in Finance

For more information about this series, please visit www.routledge.com/
Contemporary-Issues-in-Finance/book-series/CONTEMPFIN

GENDER AND FINANCE

Addressing Inequality in the Financial Services Industry

Ylva Baeckström

Routledge
Taylor & Francis Group

LONDON AND NEW YORK

First published 2022
by Routledge
2 Park Square, Milton Park, Abingdon, Oxon OX14 4RN

and by Routledge
605 Third Avenue, New York, NY 10158

Routledge is an imprint of the Taylor & Francis Group, an informa business

© 2022 Ylva Baeckström

British Library Cataloguing-in-Publication Data
A catalogue record for this book is available from the British Library

Library of Congress Cataloging-in-Publication Data
A catalog record has been requested for this book

ISBN: 978-1-032-05558-9 (hbk)
ISBN: 978-1-032-05557-2 (pbk)
ISBN: 978-1-003-19810-9 (ebk)

DOI: 10.4324/9781003198109

Typeset in Bembo
by KnowledgeWorks Global Ltd.

CONTENTS

LIST OF FIGURES AND TABLES

Figures

Tables

ACKNOWLEDGEMENTS

The list of people who have supported and encouraged me is endless. I hope you know who you are – thank you. In addition, I would like to thank the following people whose contributions and feedback on various drafts of the book have been invaluable: Mary Alexander, Kim Beauvillain, Alex Bennington, Samantha Ferreira, Piers Gibbon, Martin Gronemann, Louise Hartley, Jenni Himberg-Wild, Rita Kakati-Shah, Maria Lambides, Pui-Yee Lau, Rachel Malik, Lisa Marheineke, Wendy McCormack, Joanne McCourt, David Norman, Vanessa Nutbeam, Sophie O'Hara, Izzy Pougatch, Flo Sandelson, Jo Smith, David Sjölander, Veronica Sule, Francisca van Dijken, Tina Winter, and Sarah Woolfenden.

PROLOGUE

Imagine a world

The 2020 Gender Gap Report from the World Economic Forum[1] has just landed on your desk. You note the following as particularly interesting points:

- Across 149 countries women have on average a 31.4% advantage gap over men in the areas of economic participation and opportunity; educational attainment; health and survival and political empowerment.
- Women seem to do especially well with regards to political empowerment, where they are 75.3% points ahead of men. In economic participation and opportunity, men lag some 42.2% points behind. In this last measure, the gender inequality gap has in fact widened since the last report, further increasing women's position of advantage.
- Some 63.6% of senior private and public sector management roles are held by women. Although the gender gap has narrowed by 2% points since the previous report, this improvement is only driven by five of the participating counties. However, it is much celebrated by women on behalf of men. Progress!
- Men in OECD countries hold 22.3% of board positions. This falls to 13.8% in India and 9.7% in China.
- When women retire, they do so with a wealth of up to five times that of men and have a retirement income that is 40% higher than the male equivalent.
- In the domestic sphere, men undertake 75% of the childcare duties.[2] This is four times more than women[3] who therefore have much more time to focus on furthering their careers and pursuing their interests.
- In the most powerful and financially rewarding industry, namely, financial services, the pay gaps are the largest of all. Women are at times earning up to 66% more than men.[4]

- During its first year, the COVID-19 pandemic increased the gender inequality gap further in all areas. Men lost their jobs to a greater extent than women, and increased the hours of unpaid work they undertook including looking after the home, their children and extended families. Up to 40 years of gender equality progress was reversed during 2020.

- When complaining, men are expected to be comforted by statistics that show how patience will yield results: According to the World Economic Forum (2020)[5] they can expect to receive equal economic participation with women in just 257 years.[6] And in 107 countries, it might be sooner — a mere 99.5 years until there is at least a possibility that they will be paid similarly to women.[7]

Notes

1 The World Economic Forum (2020a).
2 Overseas Development Institute (2016).
3 Eurostat (2020).
4 Fox & Partners (2020).
5 The World Economic Forum (2020b).
6 The 2019 report stated it might take 202 years to achieve equality, the 2020 report revises that figure to 257 years. Men will need plenty of patience to get through those extra 55 years
7 The World Economic Forum (2020c).

1

GENDER INEQUALITY IS IN EVERYTHING

Readers may have already surmised that the complete opposite of the scenario painted in the prologue is true. Gender inequality means women are, and always have been, at a disadvantage to men. This inequality pervades almost everything in our society. Men have always had and continue to have an advantage over women with regards to economic participation and opportunity in every single measure available and in every country in the world. These advantages extend to the workplace where women are given far fewer opportunities to succeed because of their gender, and to the household where women adopt three-quarters of childcare duties and undertake the vast majority of domestic chores. Furthermore, in nearly all countries in the world, there is at least one article of legislation that make women's participation in the labour market more difficult.

All of this affects women financially as well as in other ways. Historically and currently, women earn significantly less than men. This tracks through into their savings and their pension pot. Ultimately, they have fewer savings to live on in their retirement when the cumulative effect of these financial problems becomes frighteningly apparent. The average woman lives 3 years longer than men[1] and yet has less to fund this longer retirement.

The financial disparities between men and women are substantial, pervade many areas and are increasing. On a global scale, whilst 78% of men have *paid* work, only 55% of women do. Women who have paid work earn on average 33% less than men.[2] When expanding the statistics to consider the annual *income gap*, i.e., that which in addition to employment income includes other income such as return on savings, assets and financial investments, the pay differential becomes much larger. While women globally have an average annual income of US$11,000, men have US$21,000. That is 65.6% more and this inequality gap is increasing.[3]

DOI: 10.4324/9781003198109-1

Removing the non-wealthy nations from the statistics and focusing instead on the 37 wealthy Organisation for Economic Co-operation and Development (OECD) countries, the numbers are slightly more encouraging but still very problematic.

Women who work earn an annual employment income that is on average 13.5% lower than that of men. This gender pay gap has decreased by only 1% point in 10 years. This is less than the average 1.5% inflation rate for the OECD countries,[4] meaning that the gender pay gap has in fact increased in real terms.

In the United States, reports show how women earn less than men at every educational level and that the pay gap increases with qualifications achieved. Whilst women without a college degree receive 23% less than their male peers, the pay differential between men and women with advanced degrees is as high as 26%.[5] So women seem to be valued less the more we need their expertise.

Women also continue to be disadvantaged in terms of access to credit or bank accounts. In 72 out of 153 surveyed countries, women belonging to certain groups do not have the legal right to open a bank account or obtain credit. In 25 countries, women do not share the same inheritance rights as men.[6] These legal challenges create barriers for women who want to start businesses, buy their own property, invest their earnings to secure their financial futures or simply participate in the financial ecosystem.

Finally, most recently, we continue to live, through the global COVID-19 pandemic. In the developed world, from a global relative perspective, the luxury of being able to work from home for many office based professions has been sought after by many people. Previously the 'jacket on the back of your chair' culture has meant that working from home has been perceived to be only for underperforming groups of people (e.g., women). Until the pandemic hit, and then it became necessary for everyone, regardless of their gender, to work from home. This challenged some of the negative gender associations previously held about women undertaking roles from home. Sadly, it has not, to date, been women who have benefitted from this.

The pandemic generally has not been good news for women in the battle for gender equality. The United Nations report that women lost their jobs at a much faster rate than men, largely due to their over representation in the hospitality and domestic services sectors. This is anticipated to contribute to an increase in the proportion of women, relative to men, living in extreme poverty – some 118 women for every 100 men aged 25–34 in 2021, rising to 121 by 2030.[7]

Furthermore, women who already performed 75% of domestic and childcare tasks, took on an increasing share of domestic duties, childcare and homeschooling responsibilities during the pandemic.

The pandemic is set to reverse years of the positive steps in the right direction for working women.

This extends to young women and girls. Data collected from families in the United Kingdom in 2021 show that a significantly higher proportion of girls than boys aged between 14 and 24 increased the work they did at home. Up to 69% of girls compared to 31% of boys increased the time they allocated to household chores, including cooking, cleaning, shopping and looking after siblings and sick relatives during the pandemic.[8] This means girls had less time than boys to focus on their education or hone their technology skills or socialise with their friends online. In the future, we will no doubt produce research about the impact this will have on the future careers and the roles of women and men in the home. Immediate impact about output is evidenced in academic professions where, for women, the negative gender gap in research outputs has increased. The share of research produced and published by male researchers increased at a higher rate than that of women. Their female counterparts produced less because more time was spent organising the domestic sphere, an experience which I share.

At the same time, a report by the European Commission in March 2021 shows how, in its first year, the pandemic worsened gender inequality in *all* areas of life despite how gender equality is a higher priority on the political agenda than ever before.[9] Clearly, the 2020 Gender Equality Strategy adopted by the Commission is not working adequately and does not translate into practice.

It is important to note that a priority is not the same as an action that promotes impactful and positive change. Across Europe, governments imposed lockdowns in an attempt to save lives. Women became less safe in their homes, with domestic violence increasing by 32% in France. (This is just one example. Several other countries saw similar increases.)

On average women spent 62 hours per week caring for children, compared to 36 equivalent hours spent by men. Women also spent 22% more time doing housework compared to men.[10] During the pandemic, one in three health ministers in the EU were women. Yet across 87 countries, men held 85.2% of the COVID-19 decision making positions.[11]

As a result of COVID-19, the choices have been taken away from many women. Someone had to pick up the additional homeschooling, childcare, cooking and cleaning. This fell on women not only because of the traditional expectations of gender roles but also because the household would lose less in economic terms by making sure that the higher earning males kept their work. Therefore, the extent of this was felt by women with successful careers in professions such as law, project management and financial services, women who also ran families. Women like these have had to resign to protect their husband's work, because it generated a higher income for the family.[12]

The pandemic continues to risk further "re-traditionalising" women back into their old-fashioned roles as homemakers with long term disadvantages and cumulative effects. Consequently, women will continue to have fewer opportunities and be poorer than men in financial terms. They have to work much harder, and be better, to achieve what they do today, handicapped by the limited resources, rights and time awarded to them. Along with doing everything else to keep the domestic ball rolling during a global crisis, working becomes more difficult and in many cases impossible.

While the move to eliminate gender inequality is ongoing, the progress towards narrowing the gap is painfully slow. In many ways, we are moving backwards in our goal of creating a society that thrives on intersectionality and allows all its participants to contribute at their full potential. The little progress made is very fragile, with the backwards movement exacerbated by the challenges of the COVID-19 pandemic.

Several factors are often mentioned, apparently serving as some sort of explanatory evidence for why men and women fulfil different roles or to justify differential treatment. Men and women *are* different, we often hear. They have different preferences and behave differently. Why try to make them the same? This is particularly challenging in business because there simply isn't a sufficient pool of women to recruit from in male dominated domains. For example, gender is thought to dictate different attitudes and behaviour towards, for example, risk-taking, educational choice and attainment levels. Someone's gender therefore determines their abilities, skill set and ultimately their ability to contribute to corporate profits or revenues. Furthermore when childbirth and child rearing make women seem more expensive to hire and less attractive as potential employees, we really need political and societal changes to right this wrong. However, these variables, used to explain the social injustice that gender inequality represents, are sometimes difficult to understand. They are not based on complete information and they don't make much sense. What is more, many of the differences that cause limitations in the opportunities awarded to men and women are caused by exclusion and gender based stereotyping. It is not about making women and men the same, the challenge is to award everyone equal opportunities to succeed regardless of who they are. We will quash many of these lazy myths in this book and we will learn how women are making important progress despite the many layers of disadvantage they have to get through before they have a chance to even get to work.

A timeline of women's exclusion from the financial system

The financial system underpins everything in every sphere. To enable full participation in a structured, modern society and the economic system that goes with it, everyone needs a bank account, access to credit and the opportunity to invest. Exclusion from the financial system is detrimental to a person's ability to progress in the formal economy.

The exclusion from granting everyone access to banking, credit and investing is still sanctioned in law. In 2014, the World Bank reported how 167 (88%) of countries still have at least one regulation that hinders the economic opportunities for women. It also noted that in 104 countries, women do not have the legal rights to work in the same way as men.[13] Although some progress has been made since then, the World Bank shows that in 2019, globally, women have just three-quarters of the legal rights afforded to men with regard to being awarded the ability to enter the workforce or start a business.[14] Sadly, its 'Women, Business and the Law 2021' study reports very little progress. Instead, it highlights the increased vulnerability for women as a result of the COVID-19 pandemic. Only ten countries – Belgium, Canada, Denmark, France, Iceland, Ireland, Latvia, Luxembourg, Portugal and Sweden – have gender equal policies. Therefore the vast majority of countries do not enable women's economic participation by law. Instead these countries have explicit gender based discriminatory practices that deliberately disincentivise women's employment and entrepreneurship opportunities. The report unearthed inequalities with relation to, for example, women's legal rights to sign contracts, apply for credit, inherit money, equally administer assets in a marriage or to take paid parental leave.[15]

> On virtually every global measure, women are more economically excluded than men.
>
> *(World Bank, 2014)*[16]

The statistics speak for themselves. In 2018, globally women were still 7% points less likely than men to have a bank account – a gender gap that has remained static since 2011.[17] In, for example India, faster progress has been made. While in 2017 only 77% of women had bank accounts, this represented an increase from 26% of women in 2011.[18] The gap is even greater in Middle Eastern and North African countries, where only 35% of women have a financial account, which is 17% points less than men. This presents a serious problem not least because banks are key to reducing poverty and increasing prosperity in developing economies. By having an account, money can be safely moved around, savings are encouraged and there are fewer barriers to access loans and insurance policies.

Needless to say, the developing world economies are regions that tend to also have other problems that are not a topic for this book. However, the developed wealthy world is not as far ahead as you might assume. It is only very recent that women were granted most of the legal rights that enabled them to participate fully in the financial systems in many developed world countries. These are economies where we tend to take it for granted that everyone has equal rights, and has had for a considerable time. However, this is just not the case.

A selection of the legal rights recently awarded to women are summarised in Figure 1.1.

FIGURE 1.1 Timeline of women's exclusion from the economic system

Source: Creation by Ylva Baeckström (2021).

Bank accounts: In 1971, 52% of women in the United Kingdom were working in paid employment, and in the United States 50% of single and 40% of married women participated in the labour force.[19,20] Yet the right for a woman to manage her own bank account was not a given. In many countries, it wasn't until the 1970s that women, regardless of whether they were working or even the main breadwinner for their families, gained the legal right to open a bank account without the application requiring a male signature too. In the United States, this right was awarded to women in 1969[21] and in the United Kingdom 1975.[22] Although it was possible for women to open bank accounts prior to these dates, the law required a man – a woman's father, brother, husband or business colleague, for example – to authorise its opening.

On Credit: women could not apply for credit to buy a home, a TV or to fund their business venture. It was not until 1974 that the Equal Credit Opportunities Act in the United States made it unlawful to discriminate against people on the basis of race, colour, religion, national origin, sex, marital status or age relating to credit transactions.[23] From that point, women in the United States became eligible to apply for credit cards. However, women in the United Kingdom had to wait until 1980 before they gained the right to apply for a credit card without a male signature.[24] This is why pioneering entrepreneurs such as the trailblazer Dame Stephanie Shirley, who started a software business in the 1960s, adopted the male-gendered name Steve for business communication and credit applications.[25] Otherwise her business would not have been able to obtain funding.

Tax matters: While completing and filing an annual tax return is a given right and independent exercise for most of us, this was not the case for women until very recently. In, for example, Sweden, a country that often sits at the top of lists of nations with the most advanced gender equality policies and progress, women weren't treated as separate tax entities from their husbands until 1971.[26] In the United Kingdom, independent taxation for spouses was introduced in 1990 when married women were granted equal opportunities which ensured privacy and independence from their husbands in their tax returns.[27]

Financial trading: Women were excluded from the ability to participate in financial trading. In the United States, it wasn't until 1967 that women were allowed to become members of the New York Stock Exchange (NYSE). Founded in 1817,[28] NYSE had already been open for business to men for 150 years. The London Stock Exchange (LSE), took even longer before admitting female members. The LSE was founded in 1698 but it was not until 1973 that the first woman was able to become a member,[29] a right that was naturally awarded to men through the opening of the exchange 275 years earlier. In other parts of the world, like India, home to the Bombay Stock Exchange (BSE), which was founded in 1876, women were first admitted in 1986.

However, for many years after granting women the right to join, male stock exchange members still controlled the admission process by being required to recommend and then approve new women members. Famously, it took Muriel

Siebert several years to fight her way to become the first female member of the NYSE in 1967.[30] She approached 10 different men before she found one to sponsor her membership. It then took her 2 years to find the money for the cost of the seat. It was eventually lent to her by Chase Manhattan bank. In India, Deena Mehta became the first female trader of the BSE in 1986 and took a seat on the board in 1996.[31]

When visiting the websites of these stock exchanges, the facts surrounding women's exclusion are excluded from their 'history' pages. This may suggest that these are considered either unimportant, or perhaps more likely, embarrassing facts for the stock exchanges.

Workplace protection: In Sweden, gender discrimination in the workplace did not become illegal until 1980[32] with The European Union Gender Equality Strategy 2020–2025 seeking to suggest policy objectives and actions that will contribute to increased gender equality across Europe.[33]

Therefore, although women were embodied in the money generating part of the financial system, they were not fully integrated, nor did they have sufficient legal rights or protection, until very recently. Instead, they were excluded from many of the rights that were so innate to men, including managing their own finances. This had the result of keeping them dependent on men to be able to conduct business and to fully participate in the economy.

What gender is

As we have seen above, women have always been, and continue to be, discriminated against because of their gender, discrimination that becomes worse for those who identify with another diverse gender. The male gender receives favourable treatment, better opportunities and higher levels of compensation for the contributions men make, sometimes sanctioned in policy. To ensure that we fully understand gender inequality and its origins, it is important to consider how gender attitudes and behaviour are formed.

It is generally accepted that people's biological sex is developed early during the prenatal environment depending on the presence of sex chromosomes (XX for females and XY for males). A baby is identified as male or female (or more rarely, hermaphrodite) evidenced by genitalia and other biological differences from the moment it draws its first breath (Hake and O'Connor, 2008). Scientists demonstrate that sex differences exist in our brains,[34] and the sex hormones *testosterone* and *oestrogen* are considered to mediate male and female behaviour. These contribute to the creation of male and female style brains, brains that are predisposed to certain behaviours. For example, higher levels of testosterone are linked to the typically male traits of aggression and competitiveness, whereas those with lower levels of testosterone tend to exhibit nurturing and caring traits associated with the female gender.[35]

However, the belief that the hardwiring of our male and female brains is determined by our biological sex and is fixed is challenged by others. Studies show that the rate of transmission of hormones is moderated by the social environment. In other words, the hardwiring in our female and male brains can be affected by our socialisation processes.[36] According to these researchers, there is a certain level of plasticity in brains which were traditionally believed to be rigidly male or female. This renders the human brain flexible and in part responsive to cultural experiences in our socialisation process.

While our biological sex is determined at birth, our gender develops as we start to interact with the world around us. Our gender association, or gender related attitudes and behaviour, is therefore culturally, rather than biologically, formed and it continues to evolve throughout our lives. Although the wiring of our female or male brain contributes to the development of whether we associate ourselves with the female, male or another diverse gender, its development is highly impacted by our experiences and exposure to outside factors.[37] This essentially means that the level of fluidity of our gender association exceeds the plasticity of our biologically sexed brains, and our gender based attitudes and behaviour are adaptable. Therefore, a person born with one biological sex may become *associated* more with another gender or indeed anywhere else along the gender spectrum

The gender based expectations held by others start from birth with parents and others in the child's social surrounding treating them differently because of their biological sex. Parents are traditionally assumed to associate behavioural differences among their children with their biological sex and treat their children accordingly.[38] Pretty much everyone reacts to us differently depending on what biological sex we were assigned at birth. Throughout the lifelong socialisation process, we exaggerate these sex and gender based differences. We form strong, often unconsciously motivated opinions about what female and what male is and how men and women should behave. Gender based biases, stereotypes and expectations are formed and these are informed by the other person's gender and our own gender.

Needless to say, there are on the female/male scale, real differences in the attitudes and behaviour of people clustered on either end of or along the gender spectrum. So, for example, an 'alpha' male is commonly assumed to be at the extreme male end of the spectrum while a feminine and caring woman finds herself at the extreme female end of the spectrum. At various other points along the spectrum, one finds alpha females, omega men, omega women and many other people regardless of their biological sex. There can be a larger distance with regards to gender based differences between an omega male and an alpha male than between a woman and a man.

People of male biological sex tend, genetically, to have more muscle mass than females. However, few men have absolutely maximised their muscle mass and few women have absolutely minimised theirs. There is stretch and flexibility within one's gender. When it comes to other traits like competitiveness or risk-taking or nurturing we are all at different points along the scale. There are few absolutes that limit us and the limits we have are only lightly bounded by the limits of our original biological sex. However, because the opportunities awarded to us in our social environment are based on our biological sex, we are not given the same chance to develop our unexpected traits. People may feel lost and misunderstood or be given derogative names if they behave in a non-gendered specific manner, for example, 'sissy' or 'butch'.

Yet at birth, we have *equal abilities* to reach our full potential. This potential is only limited by the expectations that others place on us and the expectations that we place on ourselves.

> Doing gender means creating differences between girls and boys and women and men, differences that are not natural, essential or biological.
>
> *(West and Zimmerman, 1987)*

In the socialising process, we naturally pick up on what our culture expects of us. Most of us learn to believe that being female means being more caring and careful, and that being male means being more assertive and risk taking. We learn to expect men to *naturally* run, fight and throw more powerfully than women. These gender based expectations are particularly powerful and enduring in male dominated domains, like finance.

We have the power to adjust the expectations we have of others and ourselves. All traits are available to everyone regardless of their gender. But our cultural programming is deeply embedded.

Let's consider a few examples of negative gender based expectations for context.

'Fighting like a girl', 'Throwing like a girl', 'Running like a girl' and 'Women drivers'. When reading expressions like these we tend to visualise pathetically performing women. 'Fighting like a real man' or 'Man up' create a completely different imagery, of strong, powerful men. These visuals automatically appear for most of us and have the effect of reinforcing our negative gender stereotypes.

In the case of 'women drivers', until 2018, they were banned from driving all together in Saudi Arabia. However, men cause 73% of road traffic accidents[39] evidencing that in fact, women are better and safer drivers than men. 'Manning up' suggests shutting down intelligent and healing emotional responses in favour of repressing difficult feelings. This might lead to withdrawn behaviour, resentment and future violent outbreaks.[40]

On average, people tend to adjust their attitudes and behaviour according to the expectations of others. Consider what happens to the average person who is expected to perform badly: they often do, especially if not given equal opportunities to their opposite gender counterpart.

Gender is extensively used as an explanatory variable in research studies aiming to understand how attitudes and behaviours differ among men and women.[41] There is also an increasing interest in people who identify with other diverse genders. Unless done with care, this can sometimes amplify and reinforce gender based bias and stereotypes in society so that instead of increasing our knowledge about within gender variation or the fluidity of gender based attitudes and beliefs we actually reinforce our unconscious gender based expectations.

The concept of gender is further complicated by race, socioeconomic status and other factors (Hurtado, 1997)[42] so that the gender associations are influenced by group identities, for example, white women, women of colour, men of colour and white men. The differential in power between the genders, in which men obtain the most powerful position,[43] means that there is an increased effort required by those who belong to a less powerful group as they interact with others.[44] For example, a woman of colour has an additional layer of stereotype expectations to work through than a white woman, who in turn has a less-powerful position than a (white) man.

The biologically established sex assignation and the culturally developed gender identity interact to contribute to differences in the opportunities and risks awarded to people in our society. The female sex/female gender combination is a particularly vulnerable and disadvantaged position (the World Health Organization)[45] and is one which gives rise to negative stereotypical expectations by others and indeed the expectations that women have of themselves.

It is exactly when these gender based expectations that relate to the female gender are limiting and disadvantageous to women and our society that we end up with unfair and limiting gender inequality, which sees women receiving unequal opportunities and legal rights compared to men.

However, because gender attitudes and behaviour are formed through our social interactions with others in society, we, the society, also have the power to change them. Gender is fluid and elastic. It is a cultural construct, and so we can change it. Gender in itself is not an ability moderator, but the unequal treatment of someone based on what gender they are is. That people internalise the negative projections from others and alter their feelings and behaviour is a cornerstone of psychoanalytic theory.[46] In our day-to-day life our often negative, unconscious gender based beliefs can therefore become *ability moderators* and push people into their gender expected corner.

Many of the explanations proposed to motivate, explain and continue to facilitate gender inequality are rooted in women historically being excluded from many of the rights that men have been able to take for granted and (conveniently) assigned the role of running the household and looking after children in the home. In many areas, in the 21st century, these barriers still exist, and have worsened through the pandemic. Thus, women are still predisposed to remain economically disadvantaged, and in some cases, excluded from the financial system all together.

Yet the gender associations that we make are our own fabrications and therefore gender bias and gender stereotyping are built on false pretences and unequal opportunities awarded to people because of their gender are at best bizarre. All participants in society are jointly responsible for maintaining gender inequality and for keeping the progress towards a more gender equal society slow, incremental and fragile. However, as a society we also have the power to challenge and change gender based stereotyping, and to award everyone equal opportunities to enable them to contribute at their full potential. Just writing that feels exciting for women and other disadvantaged groups. However, it is also important because our global society is much poorer in financial terms because of the limitations placed on women's potential to succeed. Allowing women to operate to their full potential as employees and consumers brings considerable advantages to our economic progress.

The power of gender inclusion

A study by the management consulting firm McKinsey revealed that allowing women to be equal to men in the labour market could contribute US$28 trillion to the global economy by 2025.[47] Considering that the global GDP was US$87.55 trillion in 2019,[48] that constitutes an additional contribution of 32% to the global economy and women's equal participation is worth roughly twice the size of China's economy.[49]

Other studies show how women are a consumer force to be reckoned with. They control up to 80% of consumer spending globally,[50] amounting to US$43 trillion in 2020.[51] Women also produced annual earnings of US$20 trillion in 2018.[52]

The financial services news and market information firm Bloomberg now describe women as 'the world's greatest emerging (growing) market'. Women's economic empowerment represents a major social change and economic opportunity.[53] The International Monetary Fund has acknowledged this by stating:

> Empowering women is also absolutely critical to achieving economic stability, to promoting growth and indeed, to transforming entire economies.
> *(IMF, 2020)[54]*

In addition, according to the World Bank:

> Legal rights for women are both the right thing to do and good from an economic perspective. When women can move more freely, work outside the home and manage assets, they are more likely to join the workforce and help strengthen their country's economies.
> *(World Bank Group President David Malpass, 2020)[55]*

Maintaining unequal opportunities which prevent women from contributing fully to society as employees and consumers is not just social injustice; it is also clearly economically harmful. According to any economic theory, that is absurd.

While arguments encouraging gender equality that promote fairness and equal opportunity may falter in some areas, the bottom line is something all businesses are quick to understand. Ironically, it may be the monetary value of women that ultimately motivates the changes that are required to achieve gender equality.

Notes

1 Statista (2020).
2 UN Women (2020).
3 The World Economic Forum (2020d).
4 OECD (2020).
5 Gogoi (2020).
6 The World Economic Forum (2020d).
7 The World Economic Forum (2020d).
8 Their World (2021).
9 European Commission (2021a).
10 European Commission (2021a).
11 European Commission (2021a).
12 Romei (2021).
13 The World Bank (2014).
14 The World Bank Group (2020).
15 The World Bank Group (2021).
16 The World Bank (2014).
17 The World Bank Blogs (2018).
18 Kohli (2018).
19 Office for National Statistics (2021).
20 Yellen (2020).
21 History Collection (2019).
22 The Telegraph (2018).
23 Rosen (2020).
24 The Telegraph (2018).
25 Shirley (2021).
26 Bremer (2021).
27 Tax and the Family (2021).
28 Osakwe (2018).
29 The Telegraph (2018).
30 National Women's History Museum (2020).
31 Wikipedia (2021).
32 Sweden.com (2021).
33 European Commission (2020).
34 Cahill (2006).
35 McLeod (2014).
36 Fine et al. (2013).
37 Hines (2011).
38 Udry (2000).
39 Brake (2020).
40 Scheff (2003).
41 Stewart and McDermott (2004).
42 Hurtado (1996).
43 Fiske (1993).
44 Frable et al. (1990).
45 World Health Organization (2021).

46 Joseph (1987).
47 McKinsey Global Institute (2015).
48 Statista (2021a).
49 The World Bank (2020a).
50 Silverstein and Sayre (2009).
51 Cision (2020).
52 Brennan (2015).
53 The Economist (2009).
54 International Monetary Fund (IMF) (2020).
55 The World Bank (2020b).

2
THE PROMINENCE AND DOMINANCE OF FINANCIAL SERVICES

The financial services industry is extremely powerful and profitable. Its influence means it can pioneer and lead gender equality to role model diverse practices in our society, practices that are economically beneficial to all.

Financial services is the business of services relating to money and investments.[1] There are a broad range of products and services, including deposits, payments, credit, insurance, financial investing, financial broking and the burgeoning financial technology that facilitates the transactions. It is a huge, evolving and powerful industry that has its fingers in every pie. It is practically impossible to live as an individual or function as a business without engaging in financial services in one way or another.

It is a substantial and growing industry. It is an industry that determines the ability for society and all stakeholders within it to operate effectively. An industry that has the ability to maintain a durable economy through the provision of stable, well-capitalised banks. It can (mostly) curb crises and thus give consumers confidence to save, raise, invest and spend money to increase their opportunities and raise standards of living. Conversely, through inadequate capitalisation, regulation and oversight, it can also be the source of economic crises, increased inequality and a widened wealth gap on individual, nationwide and global levels. Furthermore, by integrating money into the official systems, it can legitimise parts of the economy that fall outside the oversight of the government, thus reducing the black market economy. Through its payment systems and the continuing decrease in the use of cash, money is traceable and remains within the system. This benefits the nations it operates in, via tax revenues which are used by governments as investment capital and to maintain financial safety.[2]

DOI: 10.4324/9781003198109-2

It is a large, growing and profitable industry

Globally, the financial services industry was valued at US$20.49 trillion in 2020. The sector is set for impressive year-on-year growth with estimates suggesting it will grow to US$22.52 trillion by 2021 and US$28.53 trillion by 2025. The market capitalisation (the market value of all the assets) of the world's banks stand at US$90 billion.[3] This means that the value of the world's banks is greater than the world GDP, which stood at US$87.55 billion in 2019.[4]

The largest financial services markets are found in Western Europe (40%) and North America (27%).[5] Regionally, the sector continues to grow rapidly in US dollar terms.[6]

The United Kingdom is the largest exporter of financial services globally (although Brexit is likely to continue to reduce the United Kingdom's international standing). In 2019, the industry exported services worth £60 billion (approximately US$83 billion).[7] This figure rises to over £80 billion (approximately US$111 billion)[8] when surrounding facilitatory services, such as accounting and legal support, are included. The trade surplus generated from financial services revenues in the United Kingdom stands at £41 billion (approximately US$57 billion) and the industry contributed £132 billion (approximately US$183 billion) to the UK economy in 2019, amounting to 6.9% of the total economic output. Half of this was derived from London, where historically the 'City' was established as a financial centre on the north side of the Thames soon after the Roman invasion in AD50. Although financial services expanded to wider parts of London from the 1980s, the City remains a banking hub and home to The Bank of England and The London Stock Exchange.[9] In 2019, financial services contributed 10% or £75 billion (approximately US$104 billion) of the country's tax revenues.[10] Brexit remains the main threat to the financial sector, which has seen an outflow of jobs and business to European locations. Some estimates suggest that over 10,000 financial services jobs have relocated from London to overseas locations since the 2016 referendum,[11] with £5.3 billion worth of trading moving overseas on the first working day immediately after 31 December 2020.[12]

In the United States, the financial services industry generated US$1.5 trillion in 2018 or 7.4% of the US GDP.[13] US exports totalled US$114.5 billion in 2017 with a trade surplus of US$40.8 billion.[14]

In Europe (including the United Kingdom), financial services is the eighth largest industry and contributed an average 5.63% to the economy as a whole in 2019: ranging from 26.78% in Luxembourg to 2.95% in Finland.[15] The total assets owned by the five largest banks in Europe amounted to EUR9.48 billion (approximately US$11.28 billion), not much smaller than the GDP of the largest five countries in the region which stood at EUR11.43 billion (approximately US$13.61 billion).[16] In the largest European Union economy, Germany, the industry made up 4% or EUR119 billion (approximately US$142 billion) of the EUR13,928 billion (approximately US$142 billion) GDP in 2019.[17] Unlike many other industries, for example, construction or wholesale, it is also an industry that, alongside information and communication, is growing rapidly in size[18] – a trend that is expected to continue.

The Asia Pacific region is claiming an increasing slice of global GDP with its contribution rising from 24% to 31% in the ten years to 2020.[19] Although still heavily reliant on industry and the export of manufactured goods, often produced against lower ESG (environmental, social and governance) criteria than those adopted in Western economies, the region is developing rapidly with a continued rise in the middle-class population and speedy technology advances. To date the domestic financial system has been constructed to suit the industrial economy but parts of the region are also important hubs for financial trading, for example, Tokyo, Shanghai, Singapore and Hong Kong.[20] Whilst the region trails behind the Western world with regards to inclusive and equal practices, its growth is impactful and cannot be ignored. Reports suggest that in 2020, the financial services industry in Asia had a market capitalisation (market value in asset terms) that represented 37% of global figures with an increase in market capitalisation of 28% between 2007 and 2020. The continued relaxation of foreign investment in China with regards to, for example, ownership of its financial services institutions and holdings of domestic securities,[21] will sustain this accelerated growth. Such relaxation followed the same happening in India around 2012, when qualified foreign investors were allowed to trade domestic Indian securities. Such measures increase transparency and foster growth.[22]

Size in consumer terms

The consumers of financial services are all the stakeholders in our society, including individuals, institutions, governments and nations. Every single shop, hotel, restaurant, school and hospital needs some sort of financing arrangement. Every person and every legal entity in every society is either an existing or potential consumer of financial services.

Access to banking is a given in the developed world and in these high-income countries 94% of adults have access to financial accounts. This is in contrast to the global average, which, including the developing world, stands at 69%, according to the World Bank Global Findex database.[23] This was a result of how, between the years of 2011 and 2017, an additional 1.2 billion adults gained access to bank accounts which raised global participation from 62% to 69%. However, considering that 1.7 billion people still do not have access to a bank account[24] there remains a substantial growth opportunity for the reach and size of financial services.

Whilst the global average of people above the age of 15 who hold credit cards was 19.28% this rises dramatically in certain countries, such as to 82.58% in Canada.[25] Financial innovation is developing rapidly and in some countries, credit cards are swiftly being replaced by payment apps such as Alipay or WeChat (in China), or Swish (in Sweden). Over half of the transactions that take place in Europe are now cashless[26] and in the ten years to 2020, Swedes decreased the proportion of payments made using cash from 40% to 10%.[27] Sweden is set to become the world's first completely cashless society by 2023.[28] Every single transaction is routed through a financial technology system, thus increasing people's dependence on financial services as well as rapidly increasing the presence of digitalised financial services. In southeast Asia, it is estimated that revenues from digitisation will amount to US$38 billion by 2025.[29]

Globally in 2019, individuals held investments for their retirement, such as pension funds, pension insurance contracts and other products, worth more than US$50 trillion. Inequality in assets sees US$49.2 trillion of these held by individuals in OECD countries[30], another indicator of future growth potential.

Size in employee terms

The financial services industry is a large employer in which around 2% of the world's employees work,[31] and this percentage continues to grow. These employees affect the lives, opportunities and financial futures of everyone. In the United States, the industry employed 6.31 million people in 2018[32] and in the United Kingdom 1.1 million people worked in financial services in 2020.[33] People with high educational attainment from prestigious schools tend to seek out careers in financial services and these careers can be highly lucrative. For example, 28% of all Harvard graduates entered financial services in 2008 and studies show how graduates from the Stanford MBA program who entered financial services during the 1990s earned over than three times more than those who selected other industries.[34]

The potential rewards through salaries and other employee benefits are high in financial services. In fact, it is the highest paying industry by some way and was the source of fortune for 22.6% of the world's wealthiest individuals in 2019.[35]

The COVID-19 pandemic and financial services

Economic instability and uncertainty present both challenges and opportunities for the financial services industry. However, it has proved to be resilient to the COVID-19 pandemic. The need for the services it offers did not decrease during the pandemic. Instead, in many ways, they increased as consumption behaviour moved almost entirely online. Financial firms were quicker than many other industries to transition to working from home, with many introducing a week-on week-off rota a long time before lockdown became a discussion topic. In the United Kingdom, the economic output generated from financial services fell by 3% between February 2020 and November 2020. This compares to a decline in overall Gross Domestic Product of 9.9% during 2020.[36] Only 24% of firms placed staff on furlough and furlough only applied to 2% of staff compared to the 13% averaged across industries.

After an initial slowdown at the beginning of 2020, global mergers and acquisition activity increased during the last two quarters of the year, as the speed of digitalisation and business transformation become a focus for struggling and opportunistic businesses.[37]

Banks who offer services to individual customers moved swiftly into offering their services completely by electronic means. This has been so successful that many now wonder whether the transformation will become the permanent new way of operating, with relationship management remaining mainly an online activity.[38] Along with this, financial technology (Fintech) was boosted as financial services firms adapted outdated systems, increased online safety, acted against fraud and increased cyber-resilience for customers.[39] Therefore, the pandemic actually boosted Fintech deal making[40] and increased the push for innovation.

The stability of the industry during the pandemic has been attributed to the ability to adapt to flexible working. However, it is also a testament to some of the reforms, and additional capital and regulatory requirements that were introduced following the credit crisis. These ensured a presence of stable, well-capitalised banks better able to withstand crises and support the economy, rather than poorly capitalised unstable banks which themselves end up in need of support.[41]

Globally, as the impact of the pandemic lessens, the industry is set for a fast near 10% annual growth rate in 2021.

How gender equal is the financial services industry?

Gender based inequality is particularly prevalent in male dominated domains like financial services. We have seen how the financial system was created essentially by alpha males for alpha males (See Figure 1.1, Chapter 1). It was given birth to by men and assigned male biological features such as the skyscrapers that often house financial services organisations and the language such as 'generating alpha' used to describe successful performance. The financial services industry therefore has a male biological sex. By excluding women until at least the mid-1970s, it was conditioned culturally by the participants in society to develop and maintain a rigid male gender. By the industry adopting a strategy in which it seeks try to make women fit into the system rather than adapting to a more diverse community, it maintains its male identity.

So how (un)equal is it as an industry for female employees and consumers?

First, let's consider female representation in strategic, non-executive and oversight roles. The board of any organisation is responsible for holding the senior management team accountable for the way in which it operates its business and helps set and sign off on its strategic agenda. A board seat is often awarded to people because of their merit, skills and connections within a desired field. Historically, men have dominated corporate boards but in recent years, the female underrepresentation is increasingly debated and the proportion of women on boards is going up. In 2018, female board representation stood at 24.7% in the 104 financial services firms that are included in the Fortune Global 500 listing. Whilst this represents an increase of 14.4% points since 2005,[42] it is important to note that these statistics are skewed by the six French banks that are in the top ten firms with the highest female board representation. France introduced a gender board quota in 2011 which forced companies with over 500 employees or an annual turnover of EUR 50 million, to have a minimum of 40% female representation on their boards.[43] This followed a similar move by Norway in 2003. These measures have placed France and Norway ahead of the European Commission's target of 40% female board representation by 2020. In Sweden, where the proposal to fine companies that fail to meet the 40% target was rejected in parliament in 2017, women held 39% of board positions in the largest 26 banks and financial services firms in 2020. Other countries, such as the United Kingdom, recommend, rather than impose, a 30% target[44] and had 37% female representation on boards in the financial services industry in 2019.[45]

It is much less likely for a female board director to also hold an executive position. In the 104 firms surveyed above, only 14.8% of executive positions were held by women. Another study shows that only 15% of female board directors of FTSE350 listed financial services firms also hold executive management roles.[46]

At an operational level, a quick glance tells us that women are still being held back and there is a scarcity of women in senior executive roles in companies across all sectors. There are very few women who are at the helm of powerful and large organisations. In 2020, there were only 13 female CEOs of the largest 500 companies globally and only 3 of these were women of colour.[47] Looking at the commonly cited Fortune 500 companies, that is, the biggest companies measured by revenue in the United States, a record number of 37 women were in CEO positions in 2020 and only 3 of them were women of colour.[48] That means that only 2.6% of the world's most powerful and 7.4% of the most powerful US companies had women in charge in 2020 and only 0.6% of them were led by a woman of colour.

While these figures are worrying, the statistics in the financial services industry are far more alarming. The United States had 38 female bank CEOs in 2013. Five years later, there were two more bringing the total to 40. This left the (over)representation of male CEOs at 95.7%, or the proportion of female CEOs standing at 4.3%. Furthermore, these female CEOs headed up the smaller banks, usually worth US$1 billion or less. So even when women are in charge, the large banks are still run by men.

Any progress is extremely slow. While there are eight US banks that play a major role in the global banking system, none of these eight banks had ever been run by a woman until 2020 when Jane Fraser was appointed the CEO of Citigroup.[49] Of Europe's largest 25 banks (excluding the United Kingdom), only two have female leaders. These appointments took place in 2019 when Carina Akerstrom was appointed to run the Swedish Svenska Handelsbanken[50] and Kjerstin Braathen took over at the Norwegian DNB.[51]

The United Kingdom saw its first female bank CEO appointed in 2019 when Alison Rose took the helm at the UK bank the Royal Bank of Scotland. Her appointment was made within a year of RBS having fallen off the list of the world's 30 systemically most important banks.[52,53] The total assets of RBS had fallen from 2.4 trillion pounds before the credit crisis, down to 719 billion pounds.

Therefore, men led all 30 of the global systemically important banks, with the first woman appointed to lead one of them, that is, Citigroup, only in 2020. This means that 3.3%, or one, of the world's most important banks is led by a women.

Below the CEO level, in 2020 women had 36.4% representation in senior management globally across all industries.[54] However, when looking just at financial services, this falls to 20%, a small and incremental increase from 16% in 2016.[55] Female representation in management positions ranged from 34% in Australia to only 5% in countries like China and Japan.[56]

Moving down the seniority curve to junior and entry levels, we find a much higher proportion of women. In fact, women often enter the industry in similar proportions to men and frequently make up more than half of the workforce in financial services.[57] It is as seniority levels rise that these numbers dwindle.

A recent study by Catalyst – a global not for profit organisation that works with senior business leaders to build workplaces that work for women – challenges some of the ways in which the glass ceiling problem is explained. The debate often centres around how there isn't a sufficient pool of women to promote into the more senior positions because many exit the industry in their mid–30s to mid–40s which is also when the gender pay gap increases at the fastest pace. However, the Catalyst data show that women are already disadvantaged during the first promotion round. Whilst women make up roughly half of the workforce in financial services at the outset, a first round gender promotion gap sees women being 24% less likely to be promoted to the next level compared to men. This rises to 34% when comparing women of colour with white men. So even at these junior levels, 24% more men are offered career progression opportunities compared to women (or 34% relative to women of colour).[58] Thus, the talent pool is reduced very early on during women's careers. This is usually well in advance of women having children, which is often cited as the career-limiting activity for women and used as an explanatory factor for women's lesser career progression in the industry.

Furthermore, the pay gap is substantially larger in financial services than in other industries. This presents a disadvantage for women at all levels. For example, in the United Kingdom, whilst the gender pay gap was, industry wide, a shameful 17%, in 2019 women in banking earned a staggering 35% less than men. When adding bonuses, which often make up a substantial proportion of the total reward paid to senior employees in banking, women receive 59% less.[59] Across asset management groups the gender pay gap is slightly smaller with basic salaries 28.5% lower and a bonus gap of 55.4%.[60] In the United States, 2020 data show that while the average salary across financial services roles is US$91,866, the average pay for male employees was US$124,644, but women earned on average US$66,844 or 53% of what men earned.[61] This is a substantially higher figure than the national average gender pay gap of 19%.[62]

A study by the law firm Fox & Partners (2021)[63] into director pay among board directors of FTSE350 listed financial services firms demonstrates how while men are paid on average £722,000 (over US$1 million) annually, their female counterparts receive 66% less or £247,000 (just under US$345,000). Some of this is attributed to how only 15% of the female directors also hold executive management roles within their firms.

Such figures suggest that the few women who make it to the top still do not receive anywhere near the remuneration of their equally senior male colleagues. In whichever way these statistics are considered, it is obvious that the gender inequality in this well paid, powerful sector is substantially larger than in other industries.

Are female leaders in financial services represented in the media?

In September 2020, I authored together a report with Laura Jones of the Global Institute for Women's Leadership, in which we reported our findings about the visibility of women in the UK business and finance press.[64] Our report aimed to complement the analysis of the gender gap in female representation and pay in the sector, to gain an understanding of whether the women who have successful careers in the financial services industry are represented and role modelled in the written media. We analysed over 240,000 newspaper articles from *The Guardian*, *Financial Times*, *The Economist* and *City A.M.* in the period between 2014 and the end of the first quarter of 2020. Therefore, while the newspapers included in our study were UK based, we collected data about all mentions of women regardless of their nationality and country of residence. We investigated to what extent female pronouns and female opinions were reported in the press. Our findings were rather disappointing. We found that overall, by quarter 1, 2020, 18% of pronouns in the financial press were female across all articles. This remained steady when controlling for the female share of quoted speech, i.e., 'she said, she thought'. However, when controlling for 'business category articles' the female representation decreased to 15%. While the overall trend has seen an increase in female media mentions from 13% in 2014 to 18% in 2020, our report also shows that in some areas, such as female pronouns in connection with words like FTSE and retail, there has been a decrease in women's visibility, with a ceiling of around 17%.

We then narrowed the analysis down to look at notable business people (measured by the person having their own Wikipedia page). We found that only 9% of the mentions of notable business people in the financial press were of women. Clearly, the visibility of women in the business press trails their occupancy rates in senior roles in the industry. Therefore, even when women do make it, their voices are not heard. Journalists must do better. They need to find the female role models and showcase their success to the world, and organisations need to ensure that their successful women are ready for journalists and interviews. If the current pace of slow, incremental progress in women's representation in the press continues, it will take at least a further 60 years to reach equal gender representation.

Intersectionality and financial services

The injustice that is directly caused by legal exclusion and maintained through practices that are deeply rooted in gender stereotypes and gender bias is an inefficient way for our society to operate. This inefficiency, which is examined in greater depth in Chapter 5, reaches far beyond limiting women's opportunities for career progression. The financial system underpins everything in society, and an intersectional system that offers equal opportunities for financial services industry employees and consumers regardless of who they are or their backgrounds, including their sex, gender, ethnicity, race, religion or sexual preference – irrespective of whether these fit into accepted and generalisable forms – is essential. Financial services ought to be the most, not the least, equal and diverse industry of them all.

Notes

1 Cambridge Dictionary (2021).
2 The World Bank (2020c).
3 Investopedia (2020).
4 The World Bank (2020a); Statista (2021a).
5 The Business Research Company (2021).
6 International Labour Organization (2020).
7 UK Parliament (2021a).
8 The City UK (2018).
9 Investopedia (2019).
10 City of London (2019); UK Parliament (2021a).
11 Jones (2021).
12 Jones (2021).
13 Select USA (2021).
14 Select USA (2021).
15 Statista (2021b).
16 Statista (2021c).
17 Germany Trade and Invest (GTAI) (2021).
18 Eurostat (2019a).
19 Oliver Wyman (2019).
20 Statista (2021d).
21 Simmons and Simmons (2018).
22 Investopedia (2020b).
23 The World Bank (2017).
24 The World Bank (2017).
25 The Global Economy (2017).

26 Mastercard (2018).
27 Sveriges Riksbank (2020).
28 Core cashless (2021).
29 Nonninger (2019).
30 OECD (2021).
31 International Labour Organization (ILO) (2021).
32 Data USA (2021).
33 UK Parliament (2021a).
34 Oyer (2008).
35 Fraser (2020); Wealth-X (2020).
36 Office for National Statistics (2021a); UK Parliament (2021a).
37 PWC (2021).
38 EY (2020).
39 KPMG (2020a).
40 KMPG (2020b).
41 Statista (2021e).
42 Globewomen (2018).
43 Wittenberg-Cox (2019).
44 Wittenberg-Cox (2019).
45 Personnel Today (2020).
46 Data USA (2021); Fox and Partners (2020).
47 Hinchliffe (2020a).
48 Hinchliffe (2020b).
49 Citi Group (2020).
50 Handelsbanken (2018).
51 DNB Asset Management (2019).
52 Morris & Megaw (2018).
53 Financial Stability Board (FSB) (2020).
54 The World Economic Forum (2020a).
55 Catalyst (2020); https://www.catalyst.org/research/women-in-financial-services/.
56 Catalyst (2020); https://www.catalyst.org/research/women-in-financial-services/.
57 Deloitte (2019).
58 Catalyst (2020a).
59 Office for National Statistics (2019).
60 Walker (2018).
61 Data USA (2021).
62 Payscale (2021).
63 Fox and Partners (2020).
64 Jones and Baeckström (2020).

3

WOMEN AS CONSUMERS OF FINANCIAL SERVICES

Financial services is extremely powerful and profitable but remains extremely gender unequal. This is despite how women control the vast majority of consumer spending globally and are therefore very influential as consumers. However, as consumers of financial products and services women significantly trail men with regards to financial benefits. To gain further insight into why women fare worse than men in consumer terms, we will now discuss how women are treated as consumers of financial services and how women's attitudes and behaviours differ to men's when it comes to making decision about how to invest their savings.

Differences in attitudes and behaviour among men and women with regards to personal investing

It is accepted by the financial market regulators and more generally, based on prudent investment principles and economic theory derived from, for example, Markowitz (1952), Merton (1969) and Samuelson (1989), that observable individual characteristics such as age, wealth, years to retirement, personal goals and investment experience contribute to the risk preferences of individual investors. Risk, often expressed as standard deviation, is the fluctuation in the price of the assets that investors hold and therefore the possibility that returns can be positive or negative. Risk is what investors need to withstand in their quest to grow the money that they have invested to fund their retirement or meet another spending goal. This is because risky assets offer the opportunity for higher returns than almost riskless assets, such as cash.

Investment portfolios are diversified (i.e., consist of a mix of security types, such as stocks, bonds, mutual funds and cash). These securities have different characteristics with regards to, for example, risk, return and investment time horizon, and through their combination the aim is to decrease the overall

DOI: 10.4324/9781003198109-3

portfolio risk at a given level of expected portfolio return. To assist in building these optimised portfolios (portfolios that combine assets to produce the highest possible return at a given level of risk) financial market professionals and retirement fund providers may use financial modelling tools.[1] Depending on their risk and return profile, economic theory stipulates how rational investors evaluate their investment needs based on their personal situation and characteristics, to select an optimised portfolio that offers the optimal level of return given the investor's specific return requirements and ability to withstand risk (also known as their risk tolerance, risk preference or risk capacity).[2]

According to economic theory and portfolio composition theories, such as modern portfolio theory,[3] a person's *gender* does not constitute a personal characteristic that investors should take into consideration when evaluating their investment needs. Therefore, according to theory, gender neither forms part of financial modelling tools nor should it contribute to a person's risk tolerance levels.[4]

However, despite its exclusion in economic theory, research consistently presents evidence of distinct and real differences between men and women relating to investment attitudes and investment behaviour.

Women are, on average, less likely to invest compared to men. When women do invest, they prefer to invest in lower risk assets.[5] Women are also shown to feel that they have lower levels of understanding or knowledge about financial investing[6] and to be less confident about financial matters and in making investment decisions.[7] These gender differences apply both to investment attitudes and investment behaviour. Women make more conservative asset allocation decisions and hold more cash in their retirement portfolios.[8] It is therefore widely believed that women both judge themselves to be more risk averse and tend to make more conservative investment choices than men.[9]

A recent study found evidence that these self-perceptions apply not only to the average investor but also extend to women who are experienced financial services professionals. Examining the personal investment attitudes and behaviour of over 200 financial advisors I found that when comparing themselves to their male colleagues, female financial advisors consider themselves to have *lower investment risk tolerance, financial knowledge and confidence*. These women also state that they allocate a much lower proportion of their savings to high-risk assets and therefore hold assets with lower return potential.[10]

We will discuss some exceptions to these robust findings about gender differences later in subsequent chapters, but it is important to recognise that these differences are critically important and disadvantageous for women.

Research has linked them to less effective personal investment strategies which cause financial disadvantages for women and increase the gender inequality income gap for women during retirement. For example, researchers have established links between how women with low levels of investment confidence also have lower levels of risk tolerance.[11] Women lacking confidence also tend not to invest as much as they need.[12] Furthermore, women who feel they have low levels of financial knowledge tend not to hold sophisticated investment products which are likely to produce higher returns than less-sophisticated products.[13]

Statistics reveal how women are less likely to participate in retirement savings plans. This is because women, to a greater extent than men, undertake unpaid work, hold positions that do not offer retirement savings plans or which fall outside the scope of that which is covered by government pension provisions.[14] It is also more common for women to contribute to their retirement saving for a fewer number of years than men. Gaps occur usually between the ages of 25 and 44 when many women take careers breaks to look after children. This, combined with women earning much less than men during their working lives, means that the amount of money women allocate to their retirement savings is substantially lower than that allocated by men. In addition to this, women's previously noted preference for low risk investment continues into their retirement planning: They make more conservative asset allocation decisions in their retirement portfolios and hold more cash.[15] All these factors contribute to cumulative and compound effects as women have lower amounts invested in high-return assets and accrue less financial wealth than men to support their retirement.[16]

This lack of financial equality tracks a woman's whole life, with significant negative consequences. She earns less, saves less and less is contributed to her pension. The negative financial effect of being female follows her from early working life all the way to the grave.

However, this is not just down to gender preferences when it comes to investment outcomes. There is a much greater gender inequality at play. Simply considering the average gender differences in pay in the developed world creates substantial differences in the retirement savings and income of men and women. The average woman earns 17% less than the average man in the United Kingdom,[17] 19% less in the United States,[18] and 31.4% globally.[19] Pay inequality is even worse in financial services where in the United Kingdom women earn 35% less – rising to over 59% when including bonuses.

How much women and men earn during their working lives affects how much they have to live on during their retirement. For example, the retirement income difference between an average earning woman and an average earning man in the United Kingdom who both save 8% of their earnings[20] towards their retirement is over 26%. This means that the gender difference in income rises from 17% to 26%. If we instead consider the same scenario for a woman and a man who work in financial services, the gender employment income gap increased from 35% to 42%. These examples assume that the woman takes a five-year career break (usually to care for children) between the ages of 30 and 35, inflating the income gap. However, the examples exclude how women who return from breaks, often return to part time work, and miss out on promotions and pay rises that are awarded to those women and men who do not take career breaks.

Clearly, the retirement income suffers greatly from the differential in pay between women and men with women suffering from taking career breaks and working part time. Yet women in the developed world live on average 3 years longer than men; the average life expectancy is 79 years for men and 82 years for women.[21] Women need to accumulate more, not less, in their retirement savings pot compared to men if they are not to face a possibly impoverished old age. Yet, quite the opposite is true. While studies have shown that women's lower levels of risk tolerance may contribute to about 10% of the wealth differential accrued at retirement,[22] the gender gap in employment income, exclusion from pension plans and careers breaks during which retirement savings are paused are the main contributing factors, making up 90% of the gender gap in retirement income.

Investment decisions and behavioural biases

In reality, and regardless of their gender, individual investors are inherently biased in their investment decision making. They tend *not* to select portfolios which optimally balance risk and reward.[23] Instead, behavioural finance researchers show how people rely on their own judgements and intuitive beliefs when making investment decisions. Ill-informed decisions mean that they invest in portfolios that are far from efficient and which produce poor risk adjusted returns net of the trading fees that they pay for buying and selling securities.[24] Essentially, this means that people make irrational, rather than the rational investment decisions that the idealised decision maker described by economic theory is expected to make.[25]

Researchers have attempted to categorise what are believed to be the most common errors that individuals make when investing their money.

One such example is loss aversion which sees people having stronger negative emotional reactions to losses than gains, and so they try to avoid realising losses by selling underperforming securities.[26] Another example, and linked to loss aversion, is the disposition effect, which renders people likely to realise gains by selling high performing securities too quickly while they hold on to underperforming ones.[27] A third is herding behaviour, whereby investors follow trends in trading behaviour, and, for example, buy securities mentioned in the media[28].

Self-attribution bias makes individuals more likely to attribute positive outcomes (e.g., successful investments) to good investment decisions that they themselves made and unsuccessful investments to external causes or situations outside of their control. This makes it difficult for investors to learn from their mistakes[29] and to improve their investment outcomes. This might result in confirmation bias[30] and people holding onto their preconceived impressions about certain securities.

Individual investors with high levels of certain bias are more likely to believe that they have both superior knowledge relative to others and a belief that they can outperform the market.[31] For example, instead of buying securities for the medium to long term, overconfident investors buy and sell (trade) securities too frequently.[32] Each time they trade, they incur transaction charges that damage returns. Overconfidence is a bias that is associated more strongly with the male rather than the female gender. Investigating the stock trading patterns of over 35,000 individual investors over 6 years Barber and Odean (2001) found that the overconfident behaviour exhibited by male investors saw them trading 1.5 times more and therefore earning 1% point lower returns in their portfolios as compared to women. There is a need for further research that explores gender differences in relation to other behavioural biases and any possible solutions that can improve investor decision making.

Another, thus far, unclassified bias is 'avoidance'. This dilemma constitutes a widespread public ignorance of the importance of taking responsibility for personal finances. Relating to investing, this sees the majority of adults in our society today not investing enough to secure their income during retirement, and an avoidance of seeking out information about how pensions investing works and how large their retirement savings need to be in order to fund their desired lifestyle.[33] This avoidant behaviour is more prevalent among female than male investors.

Regardless of how women who are active investors may exhibit less-harmful biased trading behaviour than men, the problems posed by women's lower levels of confidence, knowledge and risk tolerance remain. Because they contribute to women shying away from focusing on their personal finances to a greater extent than men, with detrimental impacts on their retirement income.

This problem is not limited to women however. Over half of the working age adults in the United Kingdom feel that they do not understand enough about pensions to make investment decisions for themselves.[34] Nor do people know how much in savings they need to accumulate to have a comfortable retirement. It is rather disappointing that the industry uses overly complicated language and documentation for something that impacts every single person in our society.

In response to this I, together with an experienced financial advisor, created investment education lectures named 'Investing to secure your financial future' which were delivered in 2019 and 2020. These were intended to provide participants with knowledge and resources for creating a personal investment strategy that would see them through retirement. As part of this research project, I collected data from participants before and after attending. The data provided compelling evidence of low *self-perceived* financial knowledge, confidence, risk tolerance and motivation to focus on personal finance among participants (who were mainly women but also included men and those identifying with other diverse genders). The data also showed how accessible educational interventions can be very successful. Participating in the lecture unlocked higher motivation, confidence and knowledge among participants and many walked away with an action plan for securing their financial future. When following up with some participants six months later, I discovered that many had made progress and taken actions that they had committed to. They also reported substantially increased financial knowledge and understanding about retirement savings and reduced anxiety in relation to their personal finances. Therefore, increased financial knowledge positively contributed to alleviating anxiety and encouraged people to take responsibility for managing their personal finances.

Financial advice and gender differences

Needless to say, people in general find the investment and pension landscape complex and difficult to understand and navigate. Instead of managing their own investments, people may turn to professional financial advisors for information and advice on how best to invest their savings to secure their retirement. This could be an obvious way for women to overcome some of the negative associations with regards to investing linked to their gender. However, for a number of reasons entirely related to gender, it does not play through in this way.

Through their engagement the financial advisor and the individual investor enter into an agency relationship[35] in which the financial advisor acts as the agent who provides information and to whom the principal investor delegates some decision-making authority.[36] Before being able to provide investment recommendations, financial markets regulators require that advisors capture information about their clients, often using an investment questionnaire. This is used to agree a risk and return profile for each individual client.[37] There is no industry or country specific standard for the information that is captured but regulators, in line with economic theory, tend to require that advisors record information about, for example: their client's age, net worth, income, outgoings, dependents, prior investment experience, financial goals and capacity to incur losses in their investment portfolios. This ensures that the interests of the clients are protected and provides evidence to the regulators that the investment recommendations are suitable given their clients' characteristics and circumstances.[38]

The meetings between the advisors and their clients are also important social interactions during which the financial advisor makes assumptions about the investment needs of their clients and decides what investment options from a large universe to recommend to them. Therefore, the advisor makes a social cognitive judgement about each client and has the possibility to influence how they invest and can significantly influence the amount they have to live on during their retirement.[39]

Through their superior financial knowledge, access to information and experience, advisors are predisposed to make more rational investment decisions than their clients and reduce biased investing behaviour. Problematically, there is plenty of evidence that advisors make *biased* investment recommendations, tailoring them to also suit their own needs. For example, research shows that advisors sometimes make recommendations that aren't suitable for their clients, do not always promote diversified portfolios, encourage clients to trade more than they need and suggest they invest in products that generate high advisory fees.[40] Studies show how the portfolios held by advised individual investors may not produce higher risk adjusted returns net of fees compared to the portfolios that individual investors manage themselves.[41]

However, despite how advisors appear to make biased recommendations, an important role of advisors remains to educate their clients about the benefits and complexities of investing and encourage reluctant investors to convert their cash savings into securities that offer the potential for higher returns which grow their financial wealth.[42] Researchers show how financial advisor bias extends to gender. In my research, I have found evidence that women seeking to invest are disadvantaged when it comes to the evaluations that advisors make about their investment needs.

Advisors make *biased evaluations* (or judgements) about client characteristics relating to gender. In my research, I investigated how the judgements that financial advisors make about clients' investment needs depend on the gender of both advisors and investors. In these studies, published in the European Journal of Finance in 2018[43] and the Journal of Economic Behavior and Organization in 2021,[44] I presented 129 advisors with case studies, i.e., 'vignettes', or pen portraits that described wealthy investment clients. I altered the names (and gender) in each of the vignettes so that advisors were presented with an exactly equal male and female investor. I then showed the vignettes to a panel of advisors, asking them to recommend one of seven portfolios with risk and return varying from low to high. I also asked them to make a judgement about how knowledgeable the fictional investors were about financial investments and how much control they had over their investments. The results showed how male and female advisors judged women to have less control over their investments compared to exactly equivalent men. Advisors also considered the client scenarios, when portraying women, to have lower levels of investment knowledge. They also tended to recommend that women invest in lower risk portfolios. In particular, I found that female advisors exhibited greater levels of gender bias so they made lower estimations about the investment knowledge of the female investors and recommended that they invest in lower risk portfolios relative to their male colleagues.

Table 3.1 summarises these findings to show that overall, across all three measures, the lowest ratings were awarded to female clients by female advisors and the highest ratings to male clients by male advisors. Therefore, it is safe to conclude that while advisors of male and female genders both display gender bias towards female investors, these effects are stronger among female advisors.

In Chapter 4 where I discuss the relationship between gender and employment in financial services, I consider some of the reasons for and the impact of this bias, from the viewpoint of the female financial advisor.

However, continuing with the research from the perspective of the consumer, I then moved on to investigate how the *self-perceptive evaluations* (or judgements) that the investors made about their investment needs depend on their own gender and the gender of their financial advisor.

In a study published in the Journal of Corporate Finance in 2021[45], I collected statistics about the ratings that 500 wealthy male and female investors in the United Kingdom made about their own levels of investment risk tolerance, knowledge and confidence. I also collected information about how much the individuals held as cash savings relative to higher risk securities that also have

TABLE 3.1 Socially perceived judgements by financial advisors

	Male investor	Female investor
Male advisor **judgements**	**Highest ratings** Control Knowledge Risk tolerance	Control Knowledge Risk tolerance
Female investor **judgements**	Control Knowledge Risk tolerance	Control Knowledge Risk tolerance **Lowest ratings**

Source: Creation by Ylva Baeckström (2021).

Note: The *socially perceived judgements* that 129 male and female financial advisors make about the investment control, knowledge and risk tolerance (measured by portfolio recommendations) of equivalent male and female wealthy investors.

a higher return potential. Cash, as we know, produces at best zero return when interest rates are low. In today's environment of extremely low interest rates, negative returns are more likely, with returns being substantially below the general rise in costs, i.e., inflation. In my study, I collected data from 184 investors who managed their own investment portfolios and 316 investors who engaged financial advisors for information and investment advice.[46]

This research provided important evidence about the attitudes and behaviour of individual investors. Female investors, regardless of whether they managed their own investments or if they engaged financial advisors, indicated having lower levels of risk tolerance compared to men. These women also invested 5% points less than men, funds that were instead kept in cash savings that did not have the opportunity to generate any returns.

To analyse the effect of financial advice in more detail, I removed the self-directed investors and investigated the 316 investors who had financial advisors. This change found that investors who engaged financial advisors had higher levels of risk tolerance and invested 10.6% points more in risky assets which carry greater return and capital growth potential (and therefore held much less cash savings in their portfolios).

Looking at the gender of the financial advisor also proved important for the attitudes and behaviour of female investors. Women who engaged female advisors had higher levels of investment risk tolerance, knowledge and confidence and invested 11% points more of their cash compared to women with male advisors.

In fact the women, who were advised by women, turned out to be the overall 'winners' in all the categories measured. They had the highest average self-reported risk tolerance, investment knowledge and confidence, including men. These women also invested the most.

Taking the same stance with male investors, I found that, in contrast to the position with women, advisor gender bore no relevance at all. Men's investment attitudes and behaviour remained *stable* regardless of the gender identity of their advisor.

TABLE 3.2 Self-perceived judgements by individual investors

	Male advisor	*Female advisor*
Male investor judgements	*Confidence* *Knowledge* *Risk tolerance*	*Confidence* *Knowledge* *Risk tolerance*
Female investor judgements	*Confidence* *Knowledge* *Risk tolerance* **Lowest ratings**	*Confidence* *Knowledge* *Risk tolerance* **Highest ratings**

Source: Creation by Ylva Baeckström (2021).

Note: The *self-perceived judgements* that 316 advised male and female investors make about their own investment confidence, knowledge and risk tolerance by investor and advisor gender.

These findings summarised in Table 3.2 challenge the blanket assumption that *all* women have a lower willingness to take financial risk, expressed in more conservative choices in lottery experiments[47] and in retirement portfolios.[48] Instead, my research shows that women who are wealthy and successful may be exceptions but that those who observe women (i.e., financial advisors and others), assume that women *should* invest more conservatively. This builds on the findings by Nelson (2015). Following a review of 35 articles that documented gender based differences in risk tolerance, Nelson concluded that increased focus on the interpretation of the data reduced the gender gap in risk tolerance. It seems that academic researchers, akin to advisors, *expect* to find conservatism among women.

This suggests that women's risk tolerance is situationally – rather than universally – true for all women. My research shows that it matters how you *treat* women investors, who gives them advice and how they feel in the advice interaction. One could therefore say that women's attitudes and behaviour when it comes to investing their own wealth are more unstable than those of men and that traits such as confidence, knowledge and risk tolerance are more stable among male relative to female investors in their interactions with others.

This is in line with attribution theorists who find that observers tend to judge men to have more control over and confidence in their actions and abilities.[49]

This makes complete sense. Let's recall for a moment the brief history lesson in Chapter 1 detailing how women were excluded from opening bank accounts, applying for credit or trading in the financial markets until the 1970s and 1980s. This exclusion means that finance is still a new domain for women relative to men. It is a domain that has been available for men for generations because men were never excluded. Naturally, a person's attitudes and behaviour in a new area are likely to be more unstable. A person feels more unsure about how they should feel about it and they are more uncertain of how they should behave. If someone discourages instead of encourages them, they are more likely to quit.

That is exactly why it matters how the industry treats female investors, its most important consumers and its largest growth market. A woman has a greater need than a man to trust the advisor to dare to take the risk of investing. Perhaps unsurprisingly the press picked up on this research. Banks in a number of jurisdictions have engaged me to deliver bespoke training that addresses some of the gender bias that has been identified, to improve their success with female clients, increase their understanding of their financial advisors and to encourage underinvested women and underfunded female entrepreneurs to improve their economic outcomes.

In a joint research project with Philip Courtenay and Richard Taffler, I investigated what clients really want from their financial advisors. Analysing interviews with individual investors who were talking about the financial advice process, we found that people talked about the need to trust and feel understood by their financial advisors.

These needs were proved to be far more important to clients than the need to receive investment information, portfolio recommendations, and even the rate of return on those portfolios. The interviewees used emotional language, as opposed to only the rational words expected, when talking about their financial advisors and the process of investing their wealth. The emotional content in the interviews with female investors was higher than in the interviews with male investors.[50] Yet economic theory asserts that the financial advice and investment processes should entail rational recommendations from a rational agent and rational decisions by a rational investor.

These results are perhaps not surprising because for many, the investment decision process is fuelled with anxiety.[51] Inertia is also linked to people refraining from making active investment decisions or investing all together.[52] The tension between 'rational' analysis and 'irrational' emotional influences is what makes people biased in their investment decision making behaviour,[53] to the detriment of portfolio returns[54] and retirement income.[55]

In a therapeutic sense, close personal relationships, e.g., between parents and their children, or between two partners in a *good enough* marriage, or between friends, can act as containers for anxiety and other difficult feelings.[56] Containment is facilitated by trust.

Unsurprisingly, trust is also shown to be of importance in relationships within the professional domain. For example, the psychological contracts in the buyer-supplier relationships of large corporates are sensitive to breakdown in trust.[57] Trusted leaders have more effective teams and ethical practices.[58] Trust in the patient-physician relationship contributes to improved patient outcomes.[59] In financial decision making, trust in the financial advisor–investor relationship acts as a barometer for the likelihood of individuals receiving and following advice.[60] It is therefore possible that what people need from their advisors is an affective relationship that deals with their financial anxiety. This can be linked to psychoanalytic theories from Bion and Winnicott (1956)[61] about how relationships act as psychological containers that provide safe holding environments to manage difficult feelings about uncertainty. In this light, we can think about how the financial advisor relationship is not merely an agency relationship; clients are not only interested in returns. They also want containment, and therefore the relationship needs to satisfy a broader range of needs. Though financial anxiety is a separate construct to depression and general anxiety, financial anxiety or uncertainty is related to the avoidance of accessing financial information.[62] However, people are found to experience anxiety in relation to meeting with financial advisors,[63] anxiety which may deter them from seeking advice in the first place. Considering how women are found to feel fear when faced with risky situations (such as investing), while men are more likely to feel anger,[64] the containment and trust experienced in the relationship with the advisor might be more important for female than male investors. Female investors may need to feel safe and contained before risking their hard earned cash.

Women as a missed business opportunity

All this demonstrates how female consumers of financial services are disadvantaged compared to men. This is a lose–lose strategy, with neither women nor the financial services industry benefiting.

The financial services industry is losing out as female investors have more business to give them. They could earn more from their existing female clients by encouraging them to invest more and they can become more successful at recruiting more new female clients. Female consumers are losing out because they are not investing as much as they need to secure their retirement and are not earning as much as they should from the investments that they make. Therefore society as a whole loses out.

Readers with a keen eye might have spotted the perceptual mismatch in female investor–female advisor pairings. While I found that the lowest overall risk tolerance, knowledge and control judgements were made by female advisors for female investors, female investors report the highest risk tolerance, investment knowledge and confidence when paired with a female advisor.

Perceptual mismatches are described by attribution theorists as a disagreement between the explanations that observers make of the behaviour of others and the explanation that people make of their own behaviour.[65] The judgements that investors make of themselves, and the judgements that advisors make of them, are influenced by stereotypes (i.e., beliefs about certain groups),[66] including the group they belong to. Since stereotypes reflect the attributes of both the observed and the observer,[67] people become predisposed to expect to witness stereotypical behaviour.[68] This predisposition strengthens the stereotypical[69] and the stereotypical behaviour of the actor, in this case, the investor. Stereotype expectations and behaviour become deep-rooted reactions that occur without people's awareness, with mental processing stemming from the unconscious mind.[70]

The perceptual mismatches identified within the female–female gender combination of advisors and investors can be indicative of how some wealthy and successful women have shifted their gender stereotypical behaviour. Wealthy women have been shown to seek out one of the few female financial advisors that exist. (The coming chapter also explores this inequality in numbers.) Yet female advisors appear to be holding on to gender stereotypes to a greater extent than their male colleagues. These results may suggest that instead of observing the needs and abilities of the woman in front of them, people tend to draw on stereotype assumptions when judging them – assumptions that limit their abilities to reap benefits and make financial gains.

Notes

1 Markowitz (2010).
2 Campbell and Viceira (2003).
3 Markowitz (1952).
4 However, it probably ought to be considering how women live longer than men, earn less during their lifetime and tend to take career breaks during which saving towards retirement is often paused. This all contributes to why women need to generate more wealth than men to secure their retirement and are facts which affect financial modelling when planning funds needed for retirement.
5 Charness and Gneezy (2012); Grable (2000).
6 Dwyer et al. (2002); Lusardi and Mitchell (2007).
7 Barber and Odean (2001); Croson and Gneezy (2009).
8 Charness and Gneezy (2012); Eckel and Füllbrunn (2015); Sunden and Surette (1998).
9 Eckel and Grossman (2008); Gustafson (1998).
10 Baeckström (2021).
11 Croson and Gneezy (2009).
12 Pikulina et al. (2017).
13 Bannier and Neubert (2016).
14 OECD (2019).
15 Agnew et al. (2008); Charness and Gneezy (2012); Eckel and Füllbrunn (2015); Sunden and Surette (1998).
16 Neelakantan (2010).
17 Office for National Statistics (2021a).
18 Payscale (2021).
19 The World Economic Forum (2020a).
20 A retirement contribution rate of 8% is used because this is the rate that the UK Government imposed on most employed people in the United Kingdom, implemented between 2012 and 2018. It requires that a minimum of 8% is invested (5% by the employee and 3% by the employer). Gov.UK (2012).
21 Statista (2020).
22 Neelakantan (2010).
23 Benartzi and Thaler (2001); Kahneman (2003).
24 Benartzi and Thaler (2001); Kahneman (2003).
25 Tversky and Kahneman (1986).
26 Kahneman and Tversky (1979).
27 Shefrin and Statman (1985).
28 Kahneman and Tversky (1979); Shiller (2003).
29 Hoffmann and Post (2014).
30 Duong et al. (2014).
31 Barber and Odean (1999).
32 Barber and Odean (2000).
33 Financial Conduct Authority (2020).
34 Money and Pensions Service (2019).
35 Ross (1973).
36 Jensen and Meckling (1976).

37 Rosen and Wu (2004); Charness et al. (2013).
38 Kramer (2016); Hermansson (2018).
39 Kramer (2012); Hong et al. (2004).
40 Sappington (1991); Mullainathan et al. (2012); Inderst and Ottaviani (2012).
41 Hackethal et al. (2012); Kramer (2012); Hoechle et al. (2017).
42 Gennaioli et al. (2015).
43 Baeckström et al. (2018).
44 Baeckström et al. (2021a).
45 Baeckström et al. (2021b).
46 My research formed part of a larger survey administered in November 2016 by Compeer, www.compeer.co.uk, a benchmark and research specialist in the United Kingdom.
47 Dohmen et al. (2011); Agnew et al. (2008).
48 Sunden and Surette (1998).
49 Silvester and Koczwara (2012); Weiner et al. (1971).
50 Courtenay et al. (2021).
51 Loewenstein et al. (2001).
52 Bilias et al. (2010).
53 Kahneman and Tversky (1973).
54 Barber and Odean (2001).
55 Madrian and Shea (2001).
56 Colman (1993).
57 Hill et al. (2009).
58 Caldwell et al. (2008).
59 Rosser and Kasperski (2001).
60 Burke (2015)
61 Winnicott (1956).
62 Shapiro and Burchell (2012).
63 Gerrans and Hershey (2017).
64 Loewenstein et al. (2001).
65 Malle (2006).
66 Bodenhausen et al. (2013).
67 Campbell (1967).
68 Hilton and Von Hippel (1996).
69 Bussey and Bandura (1999).
70 Nisbett and Wilson (1977).

4

WOMEN AS EMPLOYEES IN FINANCIAL SERVICES

What is it like for female employees in the financial services today? To build an informed assessment picture, we have to consider the environment they are operating within. We have seen how society has created gender based expectations. We know that we make grand assumptions about the attitudes that women and men *should* have and how they *should* behave because of their biological sex. As we saw in the previous chapter, academic researchers from the behavioural, finance and social psychology fields are concerned with how people allow biases to interfere with their judgements, decision making and behaviour. This relates both to how we judge ourselves and how we are judged by others. We understand that people – men, women or those who identify with another diverse gender – find it very difficult to stretch themselves outside of the gender based expectations, expectations that include interpersonal (socially perceived) and intrapersonal (selfperceived) expectations. We have witnessed how this backdrop imposes limitations on women as investors (consumers) of financial services. So, it feels reasonable to expect that research will show that the same backdrop will also bring challenges for females working in the financial services industry.

Women as employees in financial services is a group for whom stereotypes are particularly powerful because it is an unusual domain within which to find women at all, particularly in senior roles. Those who observe women in the industry are predisposed to perceive what they expect to see. This causes incorrect perceptions of women employees and biased behaviour both towards women and of women themselves.[1] This, combined with outside factors such as the COVID-19 pandemic, during which women's behaviour was forced down the traditional female role paths, enforces the strength of the stereotype. That development impacts negatively on women employed in the industry. Despite how self and socially perceived knowledge, confidence and risk tolerance levels are elastic and higher for female managers and entrepreneurs compared to

DOI: 10.4324/9781003198109-4

women on average[2], these are fragile advances and women risk becoming re-traditionalised rapidly as evident during the pandemic. Perhaps similarly to how stereotypes are formed, social change might occur as women and men contribute to their own self-development and previously held beliefs are challenged. At the same time, despite an increase in female wealth, and a higher prevalence of female entrepreneurs and women in senior positions, working in financial services is traditionally a male domain with quantitative, rather than intuitive, skills-based criteria.

Perceptual mismatch

In the previous chapter, we noted that there seemed to be a mismatch, or perceptual error, between how risk tolerant, knowledgeable and confident female advisors consider their female clients to be and the judgements that those investors make about themselves. Essentially, wealthy women investors are being more underestimated by female, rather than male, advisors – highly educated and skilled women who work in financial services. But why is it that female advisors do this more than their male colleagues? To find out I collected personal information from over 200 financial advisors who attended training sessions on gender bias with me.

I asked the advisors about (a) how much of their own investable assets they have invested in risky assets, (b) their personal investment risk tolerance, (c) their investment knowledge, (d) their investment confidence and (e) how much their clients have invested in risky assets. I then analysed the responses by advisor gender. My findings were one directional and very clear. Although the female financial advisors had similar levels of education, years of work experience and other factors, their responses were lower across the board. This means that compared to their equally qualified male colleagues, female advisors experience that they know less, feel less confident about their abilities and say that they have a lower risk tolerance. They also invest less, both for themselves and on behalf of their clients. The differences are important in terms of how female advisors feel about themselves, and how they may experience themselves as underdogs compared to male advisors. As we saw in the last chapter, from the perspective of the female client, these qualities have economic consequences since female advisors may mirror their own lower risk preferences onto their clients. They also have consequences for the organisations that these women work for, because female advisors may be generating lower fees compared to their male peers.

A portrait of a woman in financial services

Over the years, there have been very few portraits of successful women in financial services. We will discuss some of them and the skills, strengths and advantages of women in finance in Chapter 5. However, these women are hailed as superwomen in the press, making it difficult for a *normal* woman to imagine a successful career for herself. To create a portrait of what it is like for a more relatable, woman to work in the industry I use research from my lived experience of many years in the industry together with the recorded experiences of men and women who I have encountered throughout my career. Then, more specifically, I interviewed women from a range of financial services roles for this book. These are a mix of single women and married women; women with and without children who have juggled their personal lives and careers. Although these women are all different, they share having a female biological sex and identifying themselves with the female gender.

I am grateful to the women who shared their experiences with me and to respect their privacy I will keep their identities anonymous in this chapter.

The most compelling finding from my research into the lives of women in the industry is that it is a great deal harder to thrive in financial services if you are female.

This is perhaps unsurprising considering the lack of role models of female leaders or successful women in financial services and the failure to portray these women in the media. This provides opportunities for perceptual errors in the judgements that others make about women and the judgements women make about themselves. These errors are particularly hazardous for women who are consistently underestimated by others and who consistently underestimate themsleves.

The lucky female leader

Talent + hard work = a <u>lucky</u> woman.
Talent + good contact network = a <u>successful</u>, <u>powerful</u> man.

The stereotype for a leader in financial services is a white middle class male. The voices of these white men are the ones we are used to hearing, see Figure 4.1, and these are the ones that are portrayed in the media.

Women find it extremely difficult to trust their leadership skills. Despite sometimes being more qualified and better skilled than male peers, women tend to feel that they do not deserve their position. During my research, interviewees would frequently say that they 'know that others think they were only promoted to increase gender diversity, because they are a woman'. Indeed, men (and women) think that other women are not as suitable to lead as men. In the Reykjavík Index for Leadership – an index for gender prejudice that asks: 'Do you think men or women are better suited to leadership positions?' – women's suitability receives a score of 80 out of 100 in G7 nations in 2020. This score, which measures gender bias in the G7 nations, *has not improved since 2018*. What is more, the gap in the attitudes among younger men and women is larger than for older age groups. There is a 9% point gap between the attitudes of men and women in the age group 18–34, while the gap in the age group 55–65 is 7% points. Thus younger men appear more biased against female leaders than older

*"I'm sorry, Jeannie, your answer was correct, but Kevin
shouted his incorrect answer over yours, so he gets the points."*

FIGURE 4.1 Facts don't matter

Source: By Joe Dator, 5 December 2016. New Yorker. https://condenaststore.com/featured/facts-
dont-matter-joe-dator.html. Image id 143750.

men. Younger men being less progressive in their views, could potentially lead to
long-lasting effects on gender equality fed from the younger generations.[3]

The statistics speak for themselves. Regardless of how large or small the talent
pool is, people are less likely to see leadership potential in a woman than a man. A
female leader in banking and finance does not conform to our current conscious
or subconscious expectations. Our stereotypical belief is that leadership is suited
to masculine behaviour and that leads to gender bias. Women are considered too
delicate to lead and a woman's leadership style is more likely to be considered to
be inappropriate compared to a man's.[4] Women are perceived by others as not
fitting in, and women feel this. The experience of being promoted can be fuelled
with concern about what others might think. Women I spoke to worry that their
colleagues think they received their promotion simply *because* they are women
and the firm needed to meet its diversity and inclusion targets – not because they
deserved it based on performance and future potential. Their concerns were
based on anxiety about not being good enough, and also on hearing colleagues
talk about other women's promotions through this way.

I have comforted many women whose rise in the ranks in financial services
has been filled with concern about how the promotion criteria are male skewed

and who fear the judgements of others. Precisely because of the rarity of female leaders, female leadership style is not something that anyone is used to, nor is it something that we can easily picture in our minds. In addition to stemming from outside and inside herself, the pressure comes from below and above women. Her manager is likely to question and scrutinise her leadership more because no one has a blueprint for what a female leader should be like. Others, including partners home in many cases, do the same and women internalise these gender limiting expectations. The token appointment, where a senior manager places a woman in what is often a newly created senior role to boost the gender statistics, is not helpful. This appointment is often made without a proper role definition and with no real investment into the development of the appointee. If the woman fails in the role, expectations are met, and the senior manager is let off the hook for future hires. An example exactly like this was brought to me by a male interviewee who said that the bank manager 'ticked the box' of increasing the number of female leaders in his business unit but after she 'failed' (was set up to fail), he was allowed to hire a male leader.

This *lack of role models* makes it difficult for women leaders, future and current, to find their own style. Instead, *perceptual stress* means women waste an incredible amount of time worrying about how they come across. How should she draft the email not to be misunderstood; what should she wear that is feminine, yet not too revealing; how does she walk into a room; how does she find her voice in a meeting? From my interviews, I can conclude that women spend substantially 80% more time worrying about how they come across than men do.

My research shows that to be given an opportunity a woman needs to be exceptionally good. If you are a man, employers are much more likely to take a chance on you, *they see potential because they expect potential*. Women tell me that they often feel the expectation was that they would fail, not succeed. This is sometimes very subtle but if you feel it constantly, it eventually finds a way inside your subconscious and it eats away at your confidence.

Women, who relatively speaking are better organisers and multi-taskers than men, find it all too easy to get caught into becoming the *efficient* worker who gets all the jobs done, including the work that should have been done by others. It is automatically assumed that the female in a team gets more stuff done, including organising social events, buying birthday presents and finding the time to listen to the problems of and comforting colleagues. Although this organised multi-tasking behaviour is extremely useful and can make a woman a popular colleague who gets to keep her job, it is not the sort of behaviour that receives promotions. Nor does being supportive, considerate or even collaborative. Instead, these behaviours are not rewarded properly and hinder women from finding time to focus on the big picture and to think and talk strategy. Promotions come with the closing of big deals, taking the credit for them and leaving others to pick up the pieces and do the boring jobs.

What this means is that that the closer a woman's character is to the alpha male character, the more likely she is to succeed. The *confidence* that exudes from the

"Let me interrupt your expertise with my confidence."

FIGURE 4.2 Expertise interrupted

Source: By Jason Adam Katzensteins, 15 January, 2018. Instagram image. New Yorker; https:// condenaststore.com/featured/expertise-interrupted-jason-adam-katzenstein.html

homogeneous male leader is powerful and it encourages us to believe that he is very *competent*, see Figure 4.2. In contrast, women are considered to be insecure and therefore lacking in competence. Women feel the need to do more research, they prepare more than men to increase their confidence, and to feel less intimidated or even patronised. It is not odd that women feel this way because financial institutions are often located in massive skyscrapers with meeting rooms that have enormous windows where everything is spotless and sterile. So not in friendly and cosy environments that foster inclusivity and creativity. These office environments increase the pressure for women to look perfect which they may believe conforms to some kind of male and female stereotype of what a successful businesswoman look like. It is firmly embedded in our culture that women ought to be desired by others in terms of their looks, and this spills over into the office. Confidence and perception were key discussion points in all my interviews. It is really difficult for women to get to grips with, and although men struggle with it to, it comes much more easily to men in finance.

The hiring process is sometimes challenging for women. Access to the industry gets harder the further you move away from the archetype of the white privately educated male.

If you are a white middle or upper class man, you can focus on business and get on with your own agenda. Those engaged in the hiring process consciously and subconsciously look for people like themselves. This homogeneity means that women's skills and abilities may be overlooked for what is perceived to be the 'best fit for the team'. That fit can be considered to be someone who shares similar interests as those already on the team.

Client fit is another issue. One of my interviewees had a client taken away from her because the view of her manager was that she didn't share their interest in motorsport. That was unimportant to the client but considered significant enough for the manager to move the account to a male colleague. When protesting and objecting to how she was being treated she was encouraged to take a sideline role. This particular, highly skilled and successful interviewee said 'she had all of her confidence beaten out of her during her career' through the 'patting on the head' culture.

Family planning complicates things for women. For some women this happens when they became mothers. That transition was certainly a career changing point for me and many of my interviewees. Gender differences and gender based expectations now became even more apparent – at work and at home. The planning and strategising that goes into the decision to try for children or not to have children are extremely stressful. Personally, as did most of my interviewees, I experienced shame and guilt around my pregnancies, and felt lucky to keep my job after having children. This burden is completely born by women. I have been given 'advice' by senior men not to have another child to protect my career and told how mothers who work cause problems both at home and in the workplace. I don't think fathers receive the same career advice. Women, like me, often step down in seniority because we need time to parent. Throughout my career, I have witnessed this time and again, and when interviewing women, I found many similar and worse stories. When they became pregnant or returned from maternity leave, their original roles were taken away from them. They were demoted or offered packages to leave when they tried to speak up about their difficulties. One woman returned early from maternity leave and used her remaining holiday entitlement to work four days per week for a few months. During this period, she demonstrated how she could produce the same results and bring in the same revenue that she previously did in her five-day week. When asking for a permanent move to a four-day week and the ability to leave 15 minutes early two days per week (making up that time and more on the other days) so that she could make the nursery pick up, her request was denied on the grounds that 'It would set a precedent for others to want to do the same'. That is a line that women in banking hear a lot. She resigned. When her client, the largest in the business area, found out how the bank had treated her, they moved their business to another bank. As a result, the bank lost revenue of several million dollars per year. She was then offered her job back on a four-day per week basis to save the client relationship but (obviously) declined. Another interviewee said that no one prepared her for the fact that one day she would have to quit her career because the hours meant she would never see her children. She was told that 'because you are now a mother it is probably easier for you to find an admin job'. No senior positions are offered on a part time or flexible basis but there is no reason why they couldn't be.

Having children is incredibly career limiting for women, but generally enhances the careers of men. If female leadership role models are unusual in financial services, leaders who are mothers are even more unusual. It was the experience of nearly all the interviewees, which is also shared by me, that most of the female senior managers they have had did not have children. One-third of the women I spoke to left their careers in financial services after having children. They didn't really want to and were all successful high performers. But they simply couldn't find a way for their contributions to be valued.

Not having children, or experiencing that having children is something you have to give up to have a career, is equally challenging for women. Childless women are often left to pick up the slack and cover periods when time off for parents is prioritised during for example school holidays and festive seasons. The childless woman's time is valued less than that of parents. People are often suspicious of her because she is not like women they are used to, and they may even pity her. The clash that can exist in the workplace, between women who are mothers and women who are not, can be complex and both are misunderstood.

The choice of life partner is extremely important for women. Having a supportive partner who collaborates with the domestic and childcare duties and who is proud of their partner's achievements was highlighted by the women I interviewed. In contrast, a non-supportive partner can be another career limitation. Successful men often make it because of the support of their wives but women often make it despite the lack of support from their husbands. This creates an even more uneven playing field for women and men. Some women rightly take partner choice seriously and I recall one young woman sharing how she decided to leave one of her exes on the basis that his attitudes towards household chores were too old fashioned and she feared this would have negative consequences for her future career and homelife.

What also became apparent is that the relationship support that provides something close to an equal share of childcare and domestic responsibilities, thus enabling women to focus on their careers in a more guilt free and less chores-heavy way, usually only happens in households where the male partner earns much less than the woman (which is rare). Here the decision of the childcare and home responsibilities splits are made through discussion and mutual agreement. In situations where the man earns more, his career dominates and she is left to carry that vast majority of domestic duties. She therefore loses out on career progression and the opportunity for higher earnings. I found that these are the women who tend to leave the industry after becoming mothers, an experience that I share. It becomes nearly impossible to manage everything at home and continue to progress in seniority. Women who do manage to continue despite the lack of support from their partners, often end up competing with men who have supportive partners at home, and therefore have more time than them to dedicate to work.

One of the key skills highlighted by my interviewees was relationship management and networking skills. The women considered themselves to have high levels of emotional intelligence. They also reported that they are much affected by who they are interacting with and how that interaction is experienced. Everyone I spoke to emphasised networking as one of the most important things for a career in financial services. However, despite their aptitude for it, networking is sometimes harder for women because the traditional ways to network in finance tend to centre around sports and male pursuits and activities during evenings and sometimes weekends. I vividly remember having to learn the 'football chat' to get on in my first job, something that was echoed by many of the women I spoke to. Clients in financial services are regularly taken to Formula 1, golf, cricket, football and other events which are often less accessible for women than men. So, women who work in a male-dominated domain are often expected to socialise in other male-dominated spaces, spaces that are often discriminatory against women.

It is true that many women make more conservative choices with their careers compared to men. However, this behaviour is often driven by a lack of confidence and from bad experiences. There is an obvious conflict for women, as they are required to think more like a man but not become one. The industry exacerbates this by sending women on assertiveness training to toughen them up. This feeds straight back into the impostor syndrome. The women feel like they need to change to fit in and then when they apply the 'toughened up' stance that they learnt on the courses, they are labelled 'angry', 'bossy', 'aggressive', 'difficult' and 'emotional'. The women in my research suggest that having a supportive mentor can be helpful to navigate the political landscape and office systems of behaviour, to weave networks and to identify an appropriate career strategy. Indeed, academic research echoes this but suggests (depressingly) that it might be important for the mentor to be male. That female employees do better with male mentors rather than female mentors[5] is linked to the fact that the male mentors are likely to be more senior and better connected within the organisation than female mentors.

Another factor for senior women is gender representation. As soon as women reach a certain seniority level, they receive requests to attend interview panels, committees and be a representative at several other engagements. This is because there is often a requirement for a woman to be present but there are very few sufficiently senior women in the pool to select from. While these are positive developments and the women I spoke to enjoy these, women in banking are overburdened by these kinds of engagements because of the under-representation of women at senior levels. This puts pressure on them and gives them less time to meet their targets or produce revenues that contribute to receiving promotions.

In financial services there is a sense that those who are very mathematical and have quantitative skills are superior to those who do not. Women can get trapped in this. One of my interviewees told me a typical story. She was an excellent 'quant', but she spent the first 15 years of her career trying to keep up with 'the real geeks' as required by her employer. Finally, after she was given the opportunity for a wider role which involved translating complex products into a language that clients felt comfortable with and interacting more with clients, she thrived. The skills combination of being an excellent product engineer and communicator is something extremely desirable in the industry, but it is worrying that this woman (and so many others) was not able to show these skills for the first 15 years of her career. Many women would have left the industry instead of hanging in there waiting to be discovered. Another woman with over 20 years' experience in senior roles, told me how her male colleague still speaks to her as if she was his daughter, using patronising tones when she asks for spreadsheet clarifications. This is an intimidating experience for anyone, often making the less confident person refrain from asking questions. The intimidation is built into the language. The words used in the industry are incredibly alpha and help to increase the feeling of non-belonging for women or indeed non alpha people. These words include but are not limited to: 'generating alpha', 'aggressive or risk averse investor', 'bull market', 'bear market', 'trading floor', 'structuring', 'collateral' and 'obligation'. There is nothing wrong with the words in themselves but one might postulate that Merrill Lynch's logo would not have been a bull (to symbolise strength and a rising stock market) if it had been designed by a woman. Nor would a falling stock market have been branded a 'bear market'. Similarly, the Barclay's logo might not have been an eagle-like bird symbol or Prudential's a sturdy-looking cliff-face.[6]

Many of the women I spoke to have been in the industry long enough to have attended at least one 'sausage fest party'. These are the annual events hosted by financial services institutions which feel like a sea of men with a few women scattered around. These can be incredibly intimidating and humiliating for women who may experience themselves as a token guest or part of a box ticking exercise, rather than a valued member of a team.

Pay is another complex issue. Women in the industry are well aware that they are paid less than men. This becomes evident when, for example, she is promoted, and she helps to recruit her replacement and he is paid significantly more for performing her old role, despite being more junior than her. It is evident when male colleagues have greater spending power and despite having wives whose work is unpaid, are able to afford private education and a lifestyle which is not accessible for a woman at the same level. One of my interviewees shared how she asked for her salary to be benchmarked against her male colleagues, and this resulted in her receiving a £30,000 (approximately US$42,000) pay rise. Other women told me how they had accidentally come across pay data in which the gender gaps were glaringly obvious. These examples provide clear evidence of substantial gender differences in pay in the sector.

Inappropriate behaviour is a minefield for women. It affects many woman in the industry and was echoed by every single woman I spoke to. It includes the language used on the trading floor and in the office, banter that goes too far and that women are expected to join in with, regardless of how derogatory it is. It encompasses being expected to take the notes or to serve the coffee during the client meetings. It moves into comments like 'a nice bit of skirt' when a woman enters the meeting room. This particular comment, which is something that one of the women I spoke to heard on a regular basis during her career, reminds me how one of my early employment contracts stipulated what colour tights women were allowed to wear in the office and encouraged women to wear skirts. It extends to being approached or touched inappropriately during work or client drinks; to being told that you are unusually attractive for a woman in the industry and it is nice that you are not one of those women who is trying to be a bloke. However, there are also worse incidents where women get confused about how they ought to behave. For example, the much more senior colleague of an interviewee was blatantly flirting with her during an event. She did not encourage or respond to his advances and was shocked when he knocked on her hotel room door later that evening to propose that they get together. She turned him (a married older man) down but was then very concerned about how the incident might affect her career. Another interviewee pointed out how 20 years ago we expected and knew that there would be inappropriate behaviour. We would encourage our female colleagues to be particularly careful with certain men and we would make sure no one was left alone in a potentially dangerous situation. Being exposed to unwanted sexual advances or inappropriate behaviour was par for the course and nothing unusual. Today, the young women expect things to be different. They are therefore more shocked and more deeply affected when inevitably it does happen. One of my interviews shrugged her shoulders and confirmed that she received inappropriate sexual comments or advances every single day of her 20-year career: 'That was just how it was and you just had to get on with it'. Speaking out is extremely scary and the worry about how speaking out or indeed the way women respond to advances or inappropriate behaviour will affect their careers are real concerns that take up considerable headspace, causes anxiety and again gives women less time to perform their roles.

But there were also some very good stories. Some of the women had excellent experiences around their pregnancies, maternity leave and return to work. Their *male* managers supported them, invested in them and promoted them. They tried to understand how best to support their return to work and how to support what was going on at home. They empathised, they listened and they learnt together with their high performing women. These women are still in financial services. They are very successful and their employers continue to benefit from their expertise and they speak very highly of their managers and organisations.

Women I spoke to who are at or around retirement age have seen legal reforms during their careers in the pensions, credit and tax landscape. One woman recalls how, when working part time early in her finance career, she was excluded from participating in retirement savings schemes because it only covered full time workers.

Whilst the women I spoke to acknowledge how there have been several positive developments with regards to gender equality over the last 20 years, these positive developments are now experienced to have stalled with a lot of the momentum lost. The big organisations tend to follow their more developed internal policies better than smaller organisations. There was a consensus among the women I interviewed that there has never been a better time for a woman to work in the industry. It is a much better, fairer and safer place than 20 years ago. But cultural change has slowed and even stopped. Finance bosses continue to seek out people who look and sound like them to affirm their own deeply entrenched biases. If someone agrees with their decision, they tend to think it is a good one – especially if it was reached quickly. The next stretch of this journey may well be the hardest – and yet it is needed now more than ever. Women who are currently in financial services or who are thinking of a career in the industry need to continue the work and pave the way for other women by acting as role models.

Impostor syndrome

Impostor syndrome as displayed in Figure 4.3 sees people, regardless of gender or background, questioning their abilities and feeling like they do not deserve the success attributed to them. They are more likely to attribute their competence and performance to outside factors such as luck instead of internalising these and trusting their abilities. Research demonstrates how successful people, and women in particular, are more likely to experience impostor syndrome.[7] The impostor is fiercely present among women in financial services. Women are much stronger and brighter than they themselves and others think they are. Their biggest enemy is the negative voice inside their heads, a voice that is strengthened by

FIGURE 4.3 1954: Impostor syndrome

Source: By Randall Munroe; https://xkcd.com/1954/

the negative gender based expectations of others. One experienced interviewee spoke of how she finally felt she was reaching the end of the journey of 'matching the inside with the outside', after suffering badly from impostor syndrome developed through her 20-year career in the industry.

The perception (of self and others) that female soft skills are not vital for business is nonsensical as we will see in the next chapter. As a fellow sufferer from the impostor syndrome, I am aware that we cannot control how everyone reacts to us, instead we need to be *confident* that our skills are much needed. But women tend to underestimate their abilities by up to 30% whereas men overestimate what they can achieve.[8] That, combined with how we admire assertiveness in men more than in women, make it much harder for women themselves and those who judge them to believe that they are extremely capable. However, the biggest risk is not trying, not daring yourself to go for what you really want. This behaviour will result in regret and missed opportunities for women, business and society. Women need to challenge themselves constantly to do things that feel scary, things that may appear to be, but are not actually, dangerous.

Believing that they are qualified to be where they are and not believing the stereotypes is a tough struggle that consumes both energy and time. Women are less good than men at promoting their strengths and instead focus on their weaknesses. Successful female performance that is put down to being lucky doesn't foster confidence that it can be repeated. This strengthens instead of silences the voice inside women's heads. Women need support to silence this voice so that their potential can be reached and they can focus on their careers instead of how they come across. Women in the financial industry are suffering an unwarranted and continued confidence crisis and it is hardly surprising, given the odds stacked against them. We have to change these odds, and we can.

Notes

1 Kelley (1973).
2 Johnson and Powell (1994).
3 Kantar (2021).
4 Ro (2021).
5 Ragins and Sundstrom (1989); Scandura and Viator (1994).
6 Logomyway (2021).
7 Bravata et al. (2020).
8 Zenger (2018).

5

WOMEN DO FINANCE AT LEAST AS WELL AS MEN (DESPITE THE ODDS AGAINST THEM)

We know that it is much harder for women to enjoy successful careers for a myriad of reasons. Women therefore start from a negative. On top of this, when they actually do well, their financial reward is substantially lower than that of men. This is despite all the good intentions held by many organisations and their stakeholders, driven by the desire to improve gender equality and improve business performance.

The financial services industry has a fossilised structure that ranges from the design of the buildings that house it, to the office equipment used to support it. Study after study reaffirm how the domains of finance and investing are considered by people of all genders to be intrinsically more male than female.[1]

A look at some of the equipment that is used on a daily basis confirms this: The telephone was invented by Graham Bell in 1876[2] and the first mobile phone was produced by Motorola (Martin Cooper) in 1973.[3] Thomas Edison invented the lightbulb that allows the world to work all night inventing new things and generating new wealth.[4] The first ever 'analytical engine' was designed by the truly gifted Charles Babbage, 'the father of the computer'.[5] His machine contained the first-ever 'central processing unit'. The trend continued. Hewlett Packard was founded by two men in 1939 and the computer continued to be developed mostly by men. In 1976, Apple-1 was introduced, in 1982, IBM introduced its personal computers and at the same time the laptop was created by a man called Alan Kay. The whole history of computers has been largely male.[6]

Financial services firms are often situated in buildings reminiscent of phallic symbols. Skyscrapers were originally intended to accommodate many companies in one building. They were invented by men. The first one was designed by William Le Baron Jenney and erected in 1884–1885.[7] It is referred to as the 'father of skyscrapers'. Financial centres continue to be developed in skyscrapers

DOI: 10.4324/9781003198109-5

and centres compete for who has the biggest one. This is despite evidence that people prefer and feel more productive in low-rise buildings.[8] With a little imagination we can all envisage the phallic symbol that these buildings, samples of which are shown in Figures 5.1 and 5.2, represent.

Inside these monuments to men, the male patterns continue. The first swivelling chair was invented by Thomas Jefferson in the 1770s.[9] As they sat on these chairs, men created the culture, language, architecture and everything else to do with financial services. These chairs are only now being re-designed to allow for the shape and clothing of women.

Even tiny details like the steely surface of equipment such as laptops and mobile phones are more suited to men than women. Women's hands are up to 3°C colder than men's. This is impacted by higher levels of the blood-thickening hormone oestrogen, and because less muscle mass means less heat is generated.[10] Another skirmish in the thermostat war that rages throughout the modern office.

Nor is the structure of the working day designed with women in mind. Global trading and stock market opening hours are not conducive to family life. A shorter day would allow traders to get home earlier, something which was perhaps not prioritised by the original creators. Many roles in financial services, such as in investment banking, have incredibly long hours which make them impossible to combine with being a present parent.

The male culture is even embedded in the language. The words and language used were not invented by women and reflect the alpha male culture expected to prevail in financial services for decades.

FIGURE 5.1 Chicago skyscrapers

Source: Photo 36833245 © Jesse Kraft, Dreamstime.com

FIGURE 5.2 The Gherkin, London

Source: Photo 28943203 © Dan Breckwoldt, Dreamstime.com

Women were just as intelligent and competent when the financial industry was being created as they are today, but because women were essentially excluded from the business of inventing things and excluded from the business of business itself, they were not part of the invention process.

These facts add some further context to how women in the industry work in an environment and with tools that were designed for men. These tools give men the best chance to succeed but disadvantage women.

Conservatism and overconfidence: The balanced approach

As discussed in Chapter 3, both individual investors and financial services professionals allow emotions and heuristics to interfere when making investment decisions.[11] Despite how their superior expertise, experience and access to information ought to predispose financial services professionals to rational investment decision-making and advice-giving behaviour [12], psychological factors still influence their attitudes and behaviour. This challenges the 'rational agency' assumptions made about financial market intermediation[13], and emphasises the need to increase our understanding about *how* the attitudes and behaviour are subjectively influenced.

Overconfidence is 'the quality of being too certain of your abilities or of your chances of success'.[14] Overconfident individuals tend to overestimate their own abilities, overestimate past successes and underestimate past failures. In financial trading terms this leads overconfident traders to overestimate the return potential and underestimate the risk associated with their trading decisions. This is closely related to self-attribution bias which makes traders attribute successful trades to their own abilities, and attribute unsuccessful trades to situations that are out of their control. A trader who displays both overconfident and self-attributing behaviour believes that they can consistently outperform the market[15] and finds it difficult to learn from their past mistakes.[16] Therefore, the future trading decisions that they make are likely to be as bad as the previous ones as they continue to believe that their knowledge is superior to that of others. This trait is also linked to traders selling their well-performing investments too fast and holding on to those that are losing money for too long.[17]

What these biases have in common is that they tend to belong more to the male rather than the female end of the gender spectrum. In contrast, female bias relates to underestimating themselves in terms of knowledge and abilities as well as displaying less confident trading behaviour.[18] The negative aspects of the more conservative attitudes and behaviour identified for women when making, or avoiding making, decisions around investing their own money were previously discussed in Chapter 3. We also highlighted how this more conservative behaviour actually benefits active women investors compared to active male investors. This is because the behavioural bias of overconfidence is more disadvantageous than conservatism for stock market traders as women's portfolios incur lower trading costs.

However, not knowing everything or lacking in confidence about one's abilities are not personality traits that are celebrated in financial services. The words 'I don't understand this' feel very misplaced in a culture where quick and confident decisions dominate. Anyone who has ever worked on a trading floor with four or more computer screens on each desk is acutely aware of the speedy decision-making environment. Whilst this strategy is extremely competitive, it is inconducive to innovation or thoughtful evaluation of risk and reward. However, it is conducive to herding behaviour whereby traders intentionally or unintentionally follow the crowd and copy the direction of the trades made by other traders instead of evaluating the value or growth potential in the security they are buying. Herding sees traders react similarly or identically to public information[19] and has been linked to financial market crises. Herding therefore debilitates the operations of the financial markets.[20] Herding behaviour was also evident in the strategies employed by different nations in response to the COVID-19 pandemic. Overconfident risk taking and concentrated instead of diversified investment positions are widely considered to contribute to financial market downturns and financial crises.[21] Homogeneous decision-making culture has been criticised for its contribution to bad practices, long-term systematic malpractice and long-lasting economic problems in an industry.[22] An industry that is characterised by alpha-male-skewed overconfidence. Let's consider a few examples to give this some context.

Ponzi schemes

Let's start with female led fraudulent/overconfident behaviour. In my research I found one rare example of fraudulent female behaviour. It seems that the first known Ponzi schemes were set up by women, but unlike other schemes these preyed exclusively on women. Adele Spitzeder[23] in Germany and Sarah Howe[24] from the United States carried out ladies' deposit schemes in the late 1800s on their respective sides of the Atlantic. These offered high returns on money that they then kept themselves. However, the scam didn't receive a name until the 1920s when an Italian man called Charles Ponzi operated scams in the United States and Canada.[25] It appears that women are not given credit for good *or* bad behaviour in the financial market. They pass unnoticed. A better-known scheme is that of Bernie Madoff. Madoff was already a wealthy man in the 1980s. He had been making about US$100 million annually after building the electronic trading systems which processed a large part of the NYSE's trades. He became the chairman of Nasdaq in 1990 and then moved onto starting his own Ponzi scheme. Madoff pretended to invest money in a certain trading strategy, when in fact he simply deposited the funds. He was able to run this classic Ponzi scheme for 17 years during which he defrauded tens of billions of dollars from investors. He was eventually ordered to pay back US$170 billion.[26]. In 2018, he was sentenced to 150 years in prison which is where he died in 2021.

Barings bank collapse

In 1992, Nick Leeson was a young British man with a well-paid trading job at Barings Bank. He was inexperienced but overly confident. His overconfidence was celebrated and rewarded by his leaders, because he initially made large profits on speculative and unauthorised trades of £10 million (approximately US$13.9 million). Leeson's overconfidence was damaging enough, but when combined with an absence of internal controls and the lack of external oversight, it threatened the entire banking system. Barings made trading losses of £208 million (approximately US$289 million) in 1994 and the bank eventually collapsed.[27]

LTCM collapse

Long Term Capital Management (LTCM) was a hedge fund started by big hitting male Wall Street traders. LTCM confidently boasted about the male Nobel Prize winners who also guided its investment strategy. At its height LTCM had positions worth US$1 trillion. But overconfidence in their investment strategy led to concentration risk: overexposure to one asset, in this case, Russian government bonds. When Russia defaulted on its debt in 1998, LTCM started losing billions. To avoid an economic crisis, the US government issued a US$3.65 loan fund to liquidate LTCM in 1998.[28]

LIBOR scandal

More recently we had the London Interbank Offered Rate (LIBOR) scandal[29] in which traders at large banks fraudulently manipulated LIBOR to increase their own profits. The original 2012 whistle-blower wrote that this scam had been running since at least 1991, making it a 21-year tradition for traders to believe they could fraudulently fix the rate in their favour. Chat transcripts clearly show conversations where large rewards are promised for keeping the rate at certain levels using phrases like 'I am a *man* of my word'. The LIBOR scandal led to the banks paying fines of over US$9 billion.[30]

The credit crisis

The credit crisis was made possible through a combination of overconfident business, strategy overconfident and ill-advised political decisions, and insufficient regulatory oversight. The US policy making resulted in relaxed rules around borrowing and increased lending to households who would not ordinarily be offered financing. Financial institutions took advantage and focused on the quick money that could be made from structuring and trading mortgage debt of varying risk. Complex layers of products and legal entities in which the products were held and traded were created which hid the risk from investors, who were lured by the promise of high, risk-free returns. Instead, the high risks associated with the collateralised sub-prime debts caused a global credit and liquidity crisis. This crisis went further than many previous bank crises because it affected everyone. People lost their homes, their pensions, their savings, their jobs and through austerity measures, everyone's wealth was negatively impacted.[31]

> The credit crunch is quite literally a man-made disaster, a monster created in the testosterone-drenched environment of Wall Street and the City.
>
> *(The Guardian, 2009)[32]*

At this time in my career, I was the head of a structured products desk and made a decision to refuse permission for these types of credit-linked notes and structures to be sold to our clients. This decision was opposed internally and externally but ended up saving the bank and its clients a great deal of money. It also ensured that a reputational disaster and potential lawsuits did not occur.

I based my decision on how the returns offered by these types of structures simply seemed too good to be true. I could not understand how they were able to offer such returns and still argue that the risk were so low. I refused to join in with the sales teams at other banks who were (in my view) only pretending to understand the risks. As it was my role to understand more about the products I sold than my clients did, I was unable to justify selling them. I also remember debating the low-risk ratings awarded to the product by the ratings agencies. Despite knowing that the deals could not possibly be *less* risky than sovereign debt of stable nations, they kept rating the deals as if they were. Group thinking, herding, overconfidence and greed were the business strategies that dominated.

It seems so simple when it is written down. Because it is that simple. But at the time it was, for me and everyone else who refused to recommend the products, a time of pain and pressure, with no reward or thanks. Making 'boring' or conservative decisions is rarely celebrated, even when eventually proven right by subsequent events. Instead of making lots of money, my decision merely avoided losses and my (perceived) conservatism was criticised heavily at the time. The 2015 film, The Big Short, about the male overconfidence during the credit crisis, made US$133.4 million. When we are proven right for making good but conservative decisions, nobody asks for the movie rights to our dull but very successful stories of doing the right thing for our clients or institutions. It's not seen as a heroic triumph or a daring exploit. These are not the stories we want to broadcast, but they would be excellent role modelling examples, giving confidence to others regardless of their gender to dare to speak up. Even after the event and outside of financial services, we tend to celebrate overconfident, not rightly confident, behaviour.

The credit crisis was birthed by the failures of politicians, financial markets regulators, central banks, banks, credit-rating agencies, underwriters and the other financial services organisations. The credit crisis was also a multi-level failure of leadership. All these institutions were led by the typical male leader, surrounded by others like him in his senior leadership team. In such a culture, decisions are not questioned, because everyone thinks the same, everyone wants the same and because the team is in agreement, the leaders feel that they are making good decisions. However, while homogeneous decisions are fast, they are not necessarily good. The homogeneous culture in financial services has at last come under some scrutiny. It is now fairly clear that decisions made in a monoculture are more likely to lead to bad practices. These disasters may start as a minor problem. But long-term systemic malpractice causes long-lasting economic problems which in turn reduces trust in the system and the industry itself.[33]

Male leaders are not alone in making biased decisions, but the female biases are less hazardous to the financial system and to society.[34] One of the causes for this is possibly the (on average) lower levels of overconfidence among women compared to men. Those who are less likely to exaggerate their successes may also be able to respond to uncertainty by honestly declaring their own uncertainty. This is important because it is *over* confidence, not a *lack* of confidence, that has historically been the main problem in banking. Despite this acknowledgement there is a shortage of debate around exactly how this homogeneous decision-making culture contributes to financial crises and there is surprisingly little research about gender difference in the actual performance and behaviour of male and female leaders in financial services.

Female performance: Confidence does not equal competence

A historic perspective

That women are capable of being highly competent leaders in the financial services industry is not news. We find our first female black CEO in 1903. This was the year when Maggie Lena Walker (pictured in Figure 5.3) became the first African American woman to start a bank. This inspiring teacher and businesswoman later became the President of the St. Luke Penny Savings Bank. She promoted several other women to be directors and when the bank consolidated with others, she became the Chair of the Board.[35]

Starting this bank was an incredible achievement in so many ways. Firstly, she was a woman and secondly, she was black. And consider this: when she started her bank, women in the United States did not even have the right to open a bank account in their own name. That had to wait until 1969.[36] Starting your own bank when you don't have the right to open a bank account in your own name is incredibly impressive.

FIGURE 5.3   Maggie Lena Walker (1867–1934)

Source: By Yussuf Simmonds, 18 April 2012. https://lasentinel.net/two-black-women-who-paved-the-way.html

Keeping your own bank afloat during The Great Depression was perhaps even more impressive. This was a difficult time for business and for the world. The First World War ended in 1918, followed by the influenza pandemic immediately afterwards. We now have a greater understanding of the difficulties that caused, with today's experience of the COVID-19 pandemic. The Great Depression started with a run on the banks in 1929. Global GDP fell by 18% (compared to only 1% during the credit crisis). Stock markets went into free fall. Six hundred and fifty banks failed in the 1929 Wall Street crash. But Maggie Lena Walker's bank survived.[37] Why? The simple answer is because her bank's strategy was focused more on long-term savings rather than short-term risk taking. Why is her legacy not celebrated more?

There were other female pioneers in the United States in the late 1800s/early 1900s and all of them are worth researching[38]. Louise M. Weiser was the president of the Winnesheik County Bank in Decorah, Iowa between 1875 and 1892. Deborah Powers took over her late husband's oilcloth manufacturing business and turned it into one of the largest of its kind in the world. Having done that, she started a bank, D. Powers & Sons, in 1877. Leila Comstock became the president of the Comstock Banking Company in Green City at the age of 18 in 1892. She is the youngest woman known to have served as a bank president. Evelyn Tome became the President of the Cecil County Bank and the Elkton National Bank, Maryland around 1898. She was the first woman to have been president of more than one bank at the same time. She then used her wealth to open a school which provided free education. Mary E. Miller was the President of the Lafayette Bank and Trust Company from 1900 and the Louisville Bank from 1914. She also established a school, funded the construction of churches and ran for state office. Anna Martin was the founder and President of the Commercial Bank of Mason in Mason, Texas from 1901 to 1925. Originally from Germany, she became the first woman bank president who was from outside the United States. Before founding the bank, she had opened and run a successful store.

In those days, married women were not meant to or were even entitled to run businesses. Perhaps therefore what most of these women have in common is that they started running their banks after their husbands had died. After these success stories, spread over the last century or so, the expectation could realistically be that there was a rapid development for more female leaders in financial services with female bank CEOs in great demand. Yet this did not happen.

Where were the female bank CEOs and their badly needed skills in 2008? And where are they today?

Recall the father of the computer: Babbage. Was it really a father – or was it a mother? Ada Lovelace worked as a computer programmer back in the time of Charles Babbage, and the legitimate question must be, who did the work and who got the credit?[39]

Similarly, why did Lewis Latimore not receive any credit from Thomas Edison for the invention of the lightbulb? Lewis Latimore was the son of a former slave who invented the first lightbulb that actually worked well enough to be of any use commercially.[40] Once again, the question has to be asked, who did the work and who got the credit?

Many other very important technical inventions were made by people, including women and black women, who didn't get much time in the limelight. To name a few: 3D movies, GPS, home security systems and central heating.[41]

If you look hard enough into the history of anything world-changing you can usually find someone brilliant but excluded, who had to fight through the system to make their contribution. All too often we never even hear about them.

In many stories you can't find them, it's just white men all the way. However they were not the only ones with brains and talent. But they were the only ones awarded legal rights to conduct business.

> I am, somehow, less interested in the weight and convolutions of Einstein's brain than in the near certainty that people of equal talent have lived and died in cotton fields and sweatshops.
>
> *(Stephen Jay Gould)[42]*

Recent female performance

After a brief tour of female leadership in the history of financial services it is useful to think about female performance today. There is, perhaps unsurprisingly considering the low representation, little performance data for female leaders in financial services in the modern era. So we have to start by considering the impact of gender diversity in the wider business context.

The evidence shows that women score higher than men on leadership skills.[43] Female leaders are better at engaging those they employ,[44] and they focus better on nurturing talent which increases staff well-being, productivity and reduces attrition. Their actual performance and actual contribution to revenue in organisations are substantial and not less than that of men.[45] Companies with more than one-fifth of women on their senior leadership teams have better stock price performance[46] and diversity boosts innovation.[47] Increased gender diversity results in better performance and higher profits across a wide range of industries[48] and women bring vital new skills and perspectives to business.[49] Their long-term thinking tends to be informed more by emotional intelligence and is also more collaborative and inclusive. This means that when they are given the chance, women often outperform men even when starting from a position of disadvantage. Gender diverse firms have a competitive advantage. Every firm wants to have a competitive advantage.

When a crisis hits, women led companies and even whole countries (with female leaders) are run in a way that leads to more people being safer and more wealthy.[50] This is because women tend to decrease risk taking during periods of stress, while stress can lead to increased risk taking among men.[51] An example of this is how in 2020, RBS, led by Alison Rose, took a more cautious approach than that recommended by the male led UK Government by encouraging its staff to start to work from home earlier than other banks did during the pandemic.[52]

Increasing female representation in leadership roles is not just morally right, it is good business and a necessity to future proofing any organisation. Men and women are indeed different and combining these differences with regards to perspective, idea generation, market insights and skills improve company performance on numerous levels which challenges the homogeneous group decision-making strategy in financial services. Research shows that the overall intelligence of a group is not simply the average intelligence of its members and that the collective intelligence of a group increases when women are included. Therefore, there is no gain in creating a group formed by the most intelligent people that can be sourced. Instead, because women tend to have higher levels of social sensitivity compared to men, their inclusion in the group contributes to increasing its collective intelligence. This means that, while you can't alter the intelligence of an individual much, you can increase the intelligence of a group by increasing gender diversity, thus increasing the skills mix. This held for a range of group tasks such as brainstorming, decision making, visual puzzles and complex problem solving. [53]

That 'more women means better business' is highlighted by a 2014 report by the Anita Borg Institute. This showed how Fortune 500 companies that have at least three women in director posts have a return on capital that is 66% higher than companies with fewer female directors. These companies also enjoyed a 42% higher return on sales and 53% higher return on equity.[54] There is evidence that bringing a woman onto the board of directors or into the senior management team increases the return on assets between 8 and 13 percentage points. Furthermore, companies that have more diversity in their leadership teams have returns that are 19% points higher and EBIT scores that are 9% points higher than companies with all male teams.[55] An analysis of nearly 11,000 global publicly traded firms over 8 years show that companies with women CEOs or a female Chair of the board enjoyed 25% annual returns since 2009. That is more than twice that produced by the MSCI World (Stock market) Index. In simple terms: companies with female leaders outperform the market.

A 2014 study by Gallup compared different business units in a retail and a hospitality firm, with the results showing that gender diverse units had 14% higher average revenue and 19% higher quarterly profits than less diverse business units. In a situation where there was also high within-team engagement around diversity these numbers increase to 46% and 58%, respectively.[56] Diversity is also linked to 22% lower staff turnover rates with the more inclusive culture in gender diverse companies making it easier to recruit more diverse employees.

McKinsey use their Organizational Health Index to evaluate criteria across nine different measures: accountability, direction, coordination and control, leadership team quality, innovation, motivation, work environment and values, capabilities, and external orientation. Using these measures, it compared company performance in a 2007 survey of 60,000 employees across over 100 companies. Comparing the results with the proportion of female board directors McKinsey found that companies with at least three women directors were rated higher across all nine measures compared to firms with male only boards. In addition, they identified a 47% higher return on equity and a 55% increase in operating results for companies with higher female representation on their executive committees.[57] In their 2017 report, McKinsey illustrates how, because women leaders exhibit five of the nine leadership behaviours that are shown to improve firm performance more than men, firm performance is improved on all five measures. For example, while male leaders use *individualistic* decision making and control and corrective action more than female leaders, female leaders excel in, for example: people development, expectation and rewards, role modelling, inspirational leadership, and *participative* decision making.[58] Female leaders are therefore generally found to take a more inclusive and collaborative approach to leadership and display the skills set that is thought to be the most important to address global challenges for business and society, making leadership diversity important for companies to thrive and be fit for the future. Innovation is encouraged since staff who work in diverse organisations feel valued for their uniqueness and feel more able to share their ideas freely.[59] Gender diverse and engaged teams pay off. These positive effects are attributed to how diverse genders bring more varied ideas, take different approaches to problem solving and have more in-depth insight into the market and its customers. These teams make better decisions 73% of the time compared to only 58% of the time in all male teams. Furthermore, teams that are gender equal produce higher quality work. And gender diverse companies are 15% more likely to generate above-average revenues.[60] Companies that focus on multi dimensional diversity (that is, gender, age and race) are also more profitable and more successful in expanding their market share than traditional businesses.[61]

Other studies demonstrate how the 'psychological safety', which is a significant factor that predicts team performance in emotionally challenging and uncertain environments, is increased with a higher representation of women in the organisation.[62] This simply means that people feel safer within a diverse team. It makes them feel that they can speak up, experiment, contribute and take risks. Team confidence and efficiency also increase. Psychological safety breeds innovation and creativity – identified by Google as the most important ingredient for creating high performing teams.[63]

Whilst it is not possible to establish causality, that is to say, whether it is increasing gender diversity at senior and junior levels and ensuring team engagement that caused these improvements or whether these findings are merely accidental and point to a relationship, the numbers still speak for themselves. They highlight the need for more research that doesn't merely describe the relationship, but also investigates the real cause for change. However, I have spent my entire career in finance and now dedicate my efforts to researching gender bias in financial services and I have not yet found yet any research or report that shows a *negative* relationship between increased gender diversity and improvements across a range of corporate measures. Whether it is causal or not gender equality and diversity is robustly linked to improvements.

It makes sense for companies to mirror their market place as they are more likely to understand their customers and are therefore better at serving them and make their clients feel included and cared for. Companies that adopt these principles also become a more attractive workplace for others to join and they attract better talent. It's a virtuous circle.

Recall how female entrepreneurs were unable to obtain credit in a lawful manner until recently and how trailblazers such as Stephanie 'Steve' Shirley adopted male-gendered names to fund their businesses and be taken seriously. Female entrepreneurs now have the right to fund their businesses using their female pronouns (in many but *not* all countries) but still they don't. They are less likely to apply for credit than men because they worry that credit officers will turn their applications down. Indeed, the probability for female business leaders to be granted a business loan is lower than for male entrepreneurs who operate in the same sector.[64] This is despite how the female run businesses that *are* granted bank credit outperform male run businesses. A similar story is found for venture capital funding. Entrepreneurs (of any gender) who display typically female-gendered traits, e.g., emotions, in pitching competitions are less likely to receive funding.[65] In fact, female run businesses only receive 2% of venture capital funding,[66] a small proportion of which goes to ventures run by women of colour. Yet again businesses run by women outperform and produce higher revenues than those run by men.[67] And the return on the investments that venture capital firms make into women's businesses is higher as a result. Female-run ventures are therefore better bets both for banks and venture capital firms – still they invest much less in women. Venture capital firms are also notoriously male dominated with reports showing how up to 92% of venture capital partners are male. [68]

Through interviews with young female and male entrepreneurs in 2018 I learned that it's a lot tougher for women to be entrepreneurs, even very young women. Both genders agreed that women have to work much harder and that this isn't fair. One of the people I interviewed, a very intelligent, young, black female tech entrepreneur, told me that until she found herself in a diverse environment where she was strongly encouraged to contribute with her views, she was always quiet when asked to talk about her business. She felt that there was no point in talking when no one was going to listen anyway. This young woman said she had to work much harder to get the same recognition as the men. Despite how she had better grades (at university) and performed better, men seemed to get the credit. She constantly experienced herself as the odd one out and noticed how it was difficult for both her and others around her to focus on her business and achievements rather than her race, gender and background. Being misperceived by others caused this young entrepreneur to internalise negative gender and racial stereotypes held by those around her. A woman, particularly one from an under-represented group, has much more than her business to focus on, more stereotypes and biases to combat, before being able to focus on her business.

Female performance: Financial services

As we saw in Chapter 2, the appointments of female CEOs in the banking sector took place in 2019 and 2020 and with 2020 being a year of anomaly, it is difficult to analyse the performance contributions made by female CEOs in this short time period. There is a worrying lack of studies that map out the performance of women in the industry, studies which could provide some information on the basis for paying women less and promoting fewer women. However, drawing on the statistics from the wider business context, there is no information (certainly none that I can find) that suggests that female performance is worse at leadership or more junior levels.

For example, when the gender pay gap is considered in conjunction with the financial contributions made by men and women in business, studies show that even when revenue contributions are controlled for, women are paid less.[69] This is found among male and female sales staff of Fortune 500 companies, where women are found to be paid less despite being equally good at sales.[70] In joint research with Raul Riefler, we demonstrate how female financial brokers make larger sales which generate higher per trade commission compared to their male colleagues.[71] Female brokers therefore trade less (make fewer sales) but are more profitable per trade than their male colleagues. And yet there is a significant pay differential between female and male brokers in financial services.

Researchers have documented the performance of male and female mutual fund managers. For example, female fund managers are found to outperform their male counterparts and how they at times may adopt slightly more risk in their investment strategies.[72] Other research does not document any performance or risk differences between hedge funds managed by all female compared to all male managers. [73] Another study shows how female mutual fund managers adopt more stable and therefore less risky investment strategies than male managers but still produce equal returns.[74] However, despite their equal or superior performance, clients invest less in female led funds making their funds smaller in size. Furthermore, the funds managed by female managers receive proportionately less media attention[75] and therefore their efforts and successes are not broadcast.

From a study that uses data from all private US financial services firms with over 100 employees, and federal contractors with over 50 employees between 2007 and 2015, we learn how over 75% of the CEOs of firms in the sector that have adopted a gender diversity strategy report that it helps to improve collaboration, innovation and customer satisfaction. Diversity further enhances reputation, strengthens the brand and improves the overall business performance. Improved financial performance is particularly associated with firms that prioritise diversity in their decision making on a strategic level. Other indirect benefits include improved and less homogeneous decision making, improved employee engagement, increase in net income and earnings per share, improved risk and regulatory management, identification of excluded, diverse customer groups and business models, technological enhancements and access to financing.[76]

A 2020 study that uses a sample of 144 European financial services sector companies links increased participation of women in board director positions to better financial achievements and higher performance among participating firms.[77]

We tend to believe that someone who is competent will naturally feel and appear confident. We are therefore predisposed to assume that someone who is confident is also competent. People who lack confidence instead come across as insecure and incapable. In the financial services industry, this is maintained by the decision-making culture. But facts and figures show that we are mistaken. Those who are overly confident may be more persuasive and able to make quick decisions, but the decisions that they make are not necessarily right or even good.

In financial services someone's greatest skill can be their confidence and it is this confidence, not their ability, that creates their success. This is also evident in politics and many other professions. However, for business the most sustainable and successful strategy is to possess and display an appropriate level of confidence. That can be created in diverse teams. Paradoxically, portfolio theory and rational investment strategy decision making stipulate that holding a *diverse* set of *assets* in investment portfolios produces the highest level of return for a given level of risk. Yet we do not adopt this *people* strategy in organisations.

In my work with banks and other financial institutions, I am very interested in research projects that investigate gender based *financial performance* so that we can inform ourselves better. I continue to be surprised at how little is available. Institutions simply do not compile this sort of information which is in itself interesting. What I do know from my career and research is that the *skills* that women bring are the ones that the industry really needs and are the ones that contribute to the bottom line of the business. This became more apparent following my establishment of the Economic Equality Impact Group at King's Business School in 2020, when I hosted a series of round table sessions with female and male leaders from a range of organisations in the profit and non-profit sectors as well as representatives from policy making. During these sessions, we discussed what their strategic priorities were around gender equality and what benefits they could see from investing in diversity. This was so that we could set an inclusive research agenda. One of the quotes really stood out to me. An attendee said: 'The women can do without careers in financial services, but the industry cannot do without the talent and skills that women bring'.

During a 2021 podcast recording, I asked an MD at a large bank to describe what were the most important traits he looked for when hiring a new financial advisor. Based on his 25-year plus career, he said that the skills that were required to become really successful were as follows: Excellent relationship building and management skills; the ability to build trust and *really* listen to people; engage and empathise with people; the ability to relate to people regardless of their background; flexibility in delivery and approach to situations and people; and the ability to note and remember personal details about people. We all know from our own gendered experience, and from having read the other chapters of this book, that these are the skills and personality traits that more commonly belong to the female, as opposed to male, gender. As we have seen above, some of these skills are also the ones shown to be the attributes of successful leaders across industries and those that are more strongly associated with women leaders. What is more, these are not traits that are traditionally associated with alpha or superwomen. The average woman has these traits. A successful career in financial services is perfectly possible for a non-alpha person regardless of their gender.

Recall how my research showed that female advisors gave more conservative advice to women but also how both male and female advisors assumed that female investors had less control over their investments and were hence likely to be assumed to be more dependent on their advisors.[78] We analysed this as female advisors being too conservative with their recommendations, thus mirroring their own preferences. But this could be analysed in the opposite way: It might be that male advisors, despite assuming that female clients have less control, take advantage of this perceived dependence and recommend investments that are too risky, with male advisors therefore being overconfident. That is a framing exercise: neither too much confidence nor the lack of confidence might be ideal – but working as a team to combine our diverse skills is.

The contributions made by women in financial services and across industry sectors are undeniable and often surpass those made by men. Women manage to make these contributions despite starting from a gender relative disadvantaged position and receiving less financial compensation or recognition for their contributions. It is perception, not performance, that is the problem.

Notes

1 Baeckström (2020).
2 Britannica (2021a).
3 Britannica (2021b).
4 Britannica (2021c).
5 Britannica (2021d).
6 Zimmermann (2017).
7 Britannica (2021e).
8 Aamidor (2018).
9 Eltringham (2018).
10 Shah (2017).
11 Kahneman and Tversky (1973); Wärneryd (1996).

12 Feng and Seasholes (2005).
13 Cooper et al. (2014).
14 Cambridge Dictionary (2021).
15 Barber and Odean (1999).
16 Hoffmann and Post (2014).
17 Feng and Seasholes (2005).
18 Baeckström et al. (2021a).
19 Bikhchandani and Sharma (2001).
20 Kremer and Nautz (2013).
21 Diamond and Rajan (2009); Gietl and Kassner (2020).
22 Song and Thakor (2019).
23 Partridge (2019).
24 Howe (2021).
25 Weisman (2020).
26 Britannica (2021f).
27 The Baring Archive (2021).
28 Investopedia (2021a).
29 Investopedia (2021b).
30 Investopedia (2021b).
31 Financial Crisis Inquiry Commission (2011)
32 Sunderland (2009).
33 Song and Thakor (2019).
34 Kahneman (2003).
35 Norwood (2017).
36 Silverberg (2021).
37 History (2019).
38 Examples from The National Park Service (Walker, 2019).
39 Biography (2014a).
40 Biography (2014b).
41 Weedston (2016).
42 Stephen Jay Gould (2021).
43 Zenger and Folkman (2019).
44 Fitch and Agrawal (2015).
45 Blumberg (2018).
46 Taylor (2019).
47 Boston Consulting Group (2018).
48 Herring (2009).
49 Lagarde (2014).
50 Grounds and Haffert (2020).
51 Lighthall et al. (2009).
52 Thomas and Megaw (2020).
53 Woolley and Malone (2011).
54 Herman (2021).
55 McKinsey & Company (2015a).
56 Gallup (2014).
57 McKinsey & Company (2017).
58 McKinsey & Company (2017).
59 Gallup (2018).
60 Post (2020); Del Castillo (2020).
61 McKinsey & Company (2015a).
62 Edmondson (2020); Herman (2021).
63 Culture Plus Consulting (2021).
64 de Andrés, Gimeno & de Cabo (2020).
65 Balachandra et al. (2019).

66 Harvard Kennedy School (2021); Teare (2020).
67 Weisul (2018).
68 Abouzahr et al. (2018).
69 Joshi et al. (2016).
70 Moncrief et al. (2000).
71 Riefler and Baeckstrom (2020).
72 Bliss and Potter (2002)
73 Aggarwal and Boyson (2016).
74 Niessen-Ruenzi and Ruenzi (2018).
75 Aggarwal and Boyson (2016).
76 Tucker and Jones (2019).
77 Noja et al. (2021).
78 Baeckström et al. (2021a).

6

A GENDERED PROFESSIONAL AND FAMILY LIFE BALANCE

Gender equality in financial services cannot be considered in isolation. Nor will equality be achieved by asking the industry to be responsible for making all the change. Support structures around women and organisations need to change. The predisposing measures for bringing about change require involving policy makers and addressing family support structures. This feels reasonable because the positive impacts of gender equality are not limited to improving business performance and the lives of women. Gender equality has far-reaching and positive effects on intersectional practices, family life and society. It is not just businesses which can, will and do benefit. The impact really is society wide.

Maternity leave

The gender of parenting is obvious already in the terminology used. For example, 'maternity leave' is laden with bias. Some countries are trying to move from *maternity* to *parental* leave. That should remove some of the problem but even so bias still remains in government policy making, company procedures and societal culture.

In Chapter 1, we considered how the financial services industry was born with male biological sex and how it culturally developed a male gender, something which has been maintained to date by the participants in the industry, and more generally, by society, despite pressure coming in a variety of forms. Some ground has been given at various times in the long history of the struggle by women for gender equality, such as allowing women to have credit cards, or the celebration of the first woman on the board of a major bank. These are all positive steps, but merely a smidgen of what needs to occur to level the playing field between the sexes. That has yet to take place. For example, when the Bank of England appointed Jonathan Haskel to the monetary policy committee in 2018, he was chosen from a short list of five people, four of whom were women.

DOI: 10.4324/9781003198109-6

As a result, the bank's Monetary Policy Committee continued to have only one woman among its nine members.[1]

If we look at parenting, the complete opposite is true. Parenting has female biological sex and female gender. Babies grow inside women's bodies and it is women who give birth to babies. Initially, the infant is kept alive with breast milk from the mother. This process, evolved by nature, gives parenting its biological sex. The female gender association then continues. Culturally, parenting is associated with caring and nurturing traits, traits that are associated more with the female rather than the male gender. Considering how much of our gender attitudes and behaviours are built on false pretences, it is reasonable to conclude that the cultural development of parenting as a female-gendered pursuit is similarly elastic. This elasticity is evident through the wide variation in the parental leave policies that are in operation in different countries. They are so different that the opportunity awarded to parents amount to an international lottery. Policies vary immensely, with the most family friendly policies (and therefore the most business friendly policies) found in the Scandinavian countries. However, what nearly all parental leave policies have in common is that they exclude men, to a greater or lesser extent, from parenting. This means that most fathers do not have equal opportunities and rights to parent their children compared to mothers. Conversely, mothers are coerced into assuming the main parental responsibility and thus through legislation we reinforce and maintain the stereotype that women are better suited to parenting than men. We also create a society in which fathers (on average) feel more insecure about their abilities as parents and are made to believe that they are not as important as mothers. This is because, relatively speaking, parenting is a new domain to men. Just like finance is a new domain to women. Men have been excluded from parenting through societal expectation, government and organisational policy making in a similar way to how women were excluded from finance. Fathers are just as important to parenting as mothers. More fathering gives children a broader and richer experience in life. It cascades positively down the generations and out into wider society. More fathering shows new generations of children that it is perfectly acceptable to become whatever you want, regardless of what biological sex you were born with.

To provide some context to this we will take a brief look at some of the recent history of parental leave laws. Most developed world countries are still not offering men equal legal rights with women to take time off to parent their children. Instead, it is left up to individual companies to decide what policies they want to offer.

Yet shared parental leave has an immediate effect on parenting *and* business. Putting it bluntly, there is money to be made. The Scandinavian countries frequent the top of the global indices for family friendly policies, parental leave pay, and happy places to live. They are also some of the richest countries in the world. These are currently the best places to have and raise children, places where people are the happiest to live and where they make the most money.[2] This means that the fairest countries are also the wealthiest countries. Equality is profitable for business. Equality is profitable for nations.

Let's consider the contrast between two countries: the United Kingdom and Sweden. In Sweden, parental leave allowance, which entitles parents to share their leave when a baby is born, was introduced in 1974. Over the years, quotas were introduced to encourage fathers to take leave and offer incentives to families that share parental leave. Parents in Sweden have the right to be off work for 18 months following the birth of their baby and can receive paid parental leave of up to 480 days until the child is 12. Each parent is required by law to take at least 90 days of parental leave. Policy therefore ensures that fathers take at least 3 months off. The remaining days can be transferred between the parents or is lost unless taken. Parental leave is flexible and can, for example, be taken as half days or used to reduce working hours to accommodate the needs of the family.[3] The statistics show how in 1974 mothers took 99.5% of parental leave and fathers only 0.5%. By 2005, the fathers' share of parental leave had increased to 16% and in 2020 mothers took 70% and fathers 30% (i.e., 144 of the 480 days).[4]

In the United Kingdom, the first maternity allowance was introduced after the Second World War in 1948, but it wasn't until 1976 that mothers gained the right to keep their jobs (not their salaries), but only if they had been working for the same employer for at least 2 years. UK women have the right to take up to 52 weeks maternity leave with the first 2 weeks mandatory. Until 2015, fathers only had the right to take 2 weeks paid paternity leave. Since then, parents can share 50 of the 52 weeks of parental leave (excluding the first 2 weeks).[5] The full leave has to be taken within a year of the child being born (or placed with a family). Statistics show how the proportion of fathers taking paternity leave fell steadily over the four years until 2014/2015 when 34% of UK fathers used their right to take two weeks off with their newborn.[6] In 2017/2018 only 1% of parents participated in the parental leave scheme which granted fathers the right to share parental leave with their partners. Clearly, as seen from the Swedish participation statistics, cultural change takes time . The likelihood of UK fathers taking time off to be with their babies in 2021 is nearly as low as the level in Sweden in 1974.

Another factor is pay during the time off. In the United Kingdom, statutory maternity pay rules might mean mothers receive 90% pay during the first six weeks of their maternity leave period after which they receive the lower of GBP151.97 (approximately US$211)[7] or 90% of pay should this be less than GBP151.97. However, these rights are only granted to mothers.[8] After 39 weeks, employers are not obligated to make any further payments. To be eligible for statutory paternity or maternity pay, fathers and mothers need to have been in employment for 26 weeks before the 15th week of the baby being due. This means that the rights apply should pregnancy not occur earlier than 1 week into a role with a new employer.[9] Employers can usually reclaim up to 92% of the payments made from the government.[10] Mothers who are unemployed can seek benefits if they become pregnant.[11]

In Sweden, 80% of the salaries (capped at SEK1,012 or approximately US$121 per day or US$847 per week) of mothers and fathers is paid for 390 days after which a minimum pay of SEK180 (approximately US$22) per day, that is, US$154 per week applies.[12] If a parent does not have a salary to base their payment on, they have the right to receive SEK250 (approximately US$30) per day,[13] that is, US$210 per week. The government is responsible for the pay.

Unpaid household labour is not included in GDP calculations and therefore caring for children (or others) at home is excluded. As an overwhelming majority of this work is undertaken by women, the contributions made by women are often invisible to the economy. Essentially, women carers become cost centres, rather than contributing to raising revenues for the economy,[14] and women who undertake these roles become increasingly economically dependent on others including their partners.

Accommodating parental leave policies and government subsidised childcare provision is important because they publicly signal a government led investment into women and mothers in the workplace. They facilitate a work and family-life balance that works for families and organisations and are essential to encourage and support women in their careers. The impacts of these policies are investigated by Lambert (2008) who developed an index of government policies that affect the ability for women to balance work and family life. The study measures maternity and parental leave and childcare provision for the periods up to 2003 to show how family policy matters for women's economic and political equality. In particular, the study demonstrates how women political leaders positively impact female family friendly policies. The proportion of women in parliament was positively related to improved policy making in areas related to women's employment and empowerment in the 1980s, 1990s and early 2000s. Gender diversity in political leadership lead to improved parental leave provision and encouraged more mothers to participate in paid employment. The study concludes how there is a clear link between gender diverse political leadership, improved economic outcomes and a better work/family life balance for all.[15]

Cost of childcare

Just as unpaid household labour is excluded from the economy, that is, gross domestic product (GDP), childcare costs are paid net of employment income and their costs are not tax deductible. Full-time nursery childcare places cost around GBP1,120 (approximately US$1,557) per month or more in London. That is an annual cost of GBP13,440 (approximately US$18,682) that families have to pay for each child, out of their income net of tax. This requires a gross annual income of 15,000 pounds (approximately US$20,850) to simply pay the childcare cost for one child. However, the UK government subsidise 15 hours of childcare for 3- and 4 year olds and some families can receive 30 hours of free childcare for their 3 and 4 year olds.[16] The average salary for a woman in the United Kingdom is GBP25,336,[17] which is around US$35,217 (GBP30,525, approximately

US$42,430, for men). After paying tax, she is left with approximately 20,000 pounds (approximately US$27,800). If she then spends GBP3,000 (approximately US$4,170) for her annual travel to work, she is left with GBP3,560 (approximately US$4,948) annually after paying the nursery cost for one child. This means that the average woman, assuming she also has other costs relating to utilities, work clothes and other items, has to pay to go to work. Unless the family has a supportive network of relatives or others to help with childcare, it is not affordable for the average earning mother to work, and she is likely to exclude herself from the economy by taking up unpaid household work. If she then restarts her career after all the children are in school, she has fallen behind her male colleagues in seniority, salary and lifetime earnings potential (including her pension, see Chapter 3).

In Sweden the cost for a nursery place is maximum SEK1,510 (approximately US$181) for children up to 3 years old and SEK1,007 (US$121) per month for older children, reducing for families on lower incomes.[18]

With a month's childcare costing US$1,557 in the United Kingdom and US$181 in Sweden, the affordability for mothers, even those on low pay, is much greater in Sweden. The state subsidies that cover 92% of the childcare cost are largely offset by the income generated by working mothers. On the contrary, many mothers cannot afford to work in the United Kingdom and the government and industry suffer from losing women at crucial points during their careers and from reduced tax income.

Researchers who build the case for government action on parental leave and childcare costs, report how the high childcare costs significantly contribute to mothers having to rely on social security benefits and also hinder their ability to participate in paid employment. These impediments are directly linked to it not being economically worth it or even viable for mothers to work. Mothers are therefore, through policy making, forced to withdraw from the economy.[19,20]

Consequently, it is very challenging for many women to continue their careers in a meaningful way without interruption during the early years of childrearing. Policy change is required. Until then, despite battles fought and won to date in the drive for equal work opportunities for women, it remains the reality for many women worldwide. Rightly celebrated victories in the workplace protecting women and bringing greater gender equality, are still undermined by the inability for women with small children to build on these new opportunities.

The COVID-19 effect

By now, we are all too familiar with how the pandemic continues to have a disproportionately adverse effect on women relative to men. This negative impact has a long reach, from leadership to health and even affecting their safety in their own homes. Gender inequality significantly increased during the pandemic. Women in all parts of society were rapidly re-traditionalised into old fashioned and stereotypically female roles with researchers showing how gender roles have moved back to how they were several decades ago (Allmendinger, 2021).[21] According to the United Nations, the pandemic has 'exposed endemic gender inequality'.[22] These backward steps, which erased 40 years of forward movement in gender equality in a matter of months, happened despite the stated intentions of world leaders. The UN Secretary-General António Guterres said "We need to move beyond fixing women and instead fix our systems" and the European Commission made 'significant efforts' to implement a Gender Equality Strategy.[23] In its 'Women, Business and the Law 2021' report, The World Bank declared that the COVID-19 pandemic caused increase in global inequality has not just increased women's economic insecurity but also increased the risks to women's health and safety. Therefore, policy making that keeps women safe and encourages their economic inclusion is now more important than ever. The pandemic has unearthed how much worse certain groups of people, like women and other marginalised members of society, fare in a crisis because they start at a disadvantage.[24]

As a result of the pandemic, it is women who have lost jobs on a much greater scale than men as they retrench to look after children unable to go to school; it is women who have suffered from a rise in domestic abuse by being trapped in the home; it is women who have adopted the lion's share of domestic responsibilities. It has been a dramatic slide at a time of crisis that has eroded progress made over close to half a century. This cannot be allowed to stand unchallenged. As is always the case, it is not just women who lose out, but also the institutions they work for and society as a whole.

Women have been instrumental in the fight against COVID-19 on the frontline in the healthcare sector. Women dominate the workforce in the health and social care professions making up 70% of the global healthcare workforce[25] and nearly 90% of nurses globally.[26] However, while the service is 'delivered by women, it is led by men' as the World Health Organization puts it in a 2019 report. Despite their dominance and the obvious presence of a talent pool of qualified and high performing women, only 25% of senior roles are held by women.[27] Negative gender stereotypes and gender bias block the use of the vast talent pool of women who are available to develop and promote into leadership positions. This is detrimental to global healthcare management. The WHO shows how global health is *weakened* by losing female leadership talent because women leaders are known to expand the health agenda and work towards improved health for all. The disadvantages of the exclusion of women leaders in health became even more apparent when women were excluded from the strategic management of the global response to the pandemic. Early statistics suggest that countries with women in charge had slightly lower fatality rates than those with men in charge.[28]

In financial services, flexible working practices and working from home have always carried the stigma of being carried out by underperforming or rather undervalued members of staff. These staff members tended to be women, often mothers. Most roles were not available on a flexible or part time basis and those who asked for them were marginalised and excluded from promotion and career progression. Recall the example of my interviewee who showed she could perform her role in four days and still generate the same revenues for the bank, while accepting a reduction in her own income to the equivalent of four days pay rather than five but who was still refused part-time work. This, as we saw, led to the bank losing its largest client when she left. There has never been, to date, any consideration of the economic motivations for the stigmatisation and the resultant mass exodus of (female) talent from financial services. Instead, terms like 'we don't want to set the precedent for others' and 'if we let you do it, others might want to do the same' were commonly used – until the pandemic. When the pandemic arrived, nearly everyone in financial services *had to* work from home. Quickly, working from home became part of the strategic management of the response during national lockdowns. In financial services, working from home had the potential to create more inclusive opportunities for women, mothers and carers.

It is important to note that prior to the pandemic, women's voices were not heard, and women's needs were not met in the financial services industry. This was not limited to women and mothers. Working from home was asked for by other marginalised groups, for example, disabled people, and others for whom a commute to work is difficult for whatever reason. However, working from home did not become an acceptable practice until it was ordered by male-dominated authorities in response to a global crisis.

Sadly, following the pandemic, women have not yet become the beneficiaries of the year-long demonstration of how effective working from home can be.

There are only disadvantages with this excluding business strategy. The exodus of mothers of young children drains the talent pool of future leaders; it means banks lose revenue and business opportunities; and it continues to perpetuate negative gender stereotypes. The perception that those in financial services hold of many women and mothers is that they can't cope with the challenge of the job, so they either decide to take a part time role or leave the industry altogether. But it seems that in actual fact, it is the industry that can't cope with accommodating the women and therefore simply continues to make decisions that are based on outdated values. Decisions that aren't economically viable. No one wins.

Many banks performed exceptionally well during the pandemic. Some 2020 annual reports show how banks globally recorded healthy[29] and record profits.[30] Banks were able to profit from the increased volatility and uncertainty presented by the pandemic and did not suffer from its staff working from home. Their services carried on seamlessly and considerable time and money was saved by avoiding travel, entertainment and other activities associated with the traditional ways in which banks operate. The business strategy that women had been asking for over the years paid off. It is easy to think that women can now relax and assume that these positive developments will continue to allow us all to reap the benefits. However, in spring 2021 banks in the developed world began to voice their plans for return to office strategies. US executives announced a rapid return to pre-pandemic normality with giants JP Morgan and Goldman Sachs asking their staff to return to the office in early summer 2021. The CEO (Jamie Dimon) of JP Morgan, a US bank that recorded revenue growth of 14% in the first quarter of 2021[31], accredited these to their 'diversified business model and dedicated employees'.[32] Despite the successful business strategy during lockdown, the Financial Times reported how the CEO ordered the end to working from home and a swift return to the office, cancelling all Zoom meetings because he was 'done with it'.[33] A move that is detrimental to families and in particular women whose children had only recently returned to school following numerous closures. The statement made by Jamie Dimon that things will look just like they did before, and that JP Morgan had lost business to other banks due to not meeting clients face to face, reflects negative bias and historic strategies that risk seeing the firm return to its previous excluding practices. Similarly, in June 2021, the Financial Times reported how the CEO of Morgan Stanley, James Gorman, said 'If you can go into a restaurant in New York City, you can come into the office and we want you in the office'.[34] On the other hand, some European banks, for example, French Société Générale, announced a global strategy that would allow staff to work from home three days a week post the pandemic. The bank's CEO Frédéric Oudéa said this strategy would appeal to a young talent pool that doesn't 'see the world in the same way they did just two years ago'.[35] The CEO (Noel Quinn) of the UK bank HSBC said he would lead by example and continue to work partly remotely, reduce business travel and 40% of global head office costs.[36]

Which strategies survive remain to be seen. But the ones that are most attractive to a diverse workforce and the future talent pool are the ones that offer flexible working arrangements and a continuation of the ability to work, at least partly, remotely; that is, versions of the strategy that proved so successful during 2020 and 2021. These are also the strategies that are most economically beneficial and the most sustainable.

Positive impacts of policy making

Gender inclusive policy making relating to parental leave has a positive impact. For example, this is evident in the representation of women in senior leadership positions and in board seats.

In 2020 in the EU, 66.7% of women participated in the labour market with 29.3% of these women working part time. The female employment rate in the United Kingdom was higher at 71.8% but the United Kingdom also has a higher share of women working part time – currently the figure is 38%. This compares to only 13% of UK men work part time (House of Commons, 2021).[37] Sweden has the highest proportion of women in the labour market, 78.3% but similarly many more women than men (30%) work part time.[38]

In Sweden, the proportion of women in middle to senior management positions (36.3%) nearly mirrors the proportion of women in the workplace as a whole (37.8%). In this middle to senior leadership segment 39% of the managers appointed in 2018–2019 were women and[39] on average 17% of CEOs in Sweden were women in 2019.[40] The equivalent number in the United Kingdom was 27.9% of women with direct line management responsibilities in the FTSE 250 companies in 2018–2019. [41] In the same sample of companies, 18.6% of executive positions were held by women and only 3.2% of CEOs were women. In Sweden, 38% of board seats were occupied by women in 2020,[42] higher than the EU and UK average of around 30%.[43]

These differences in gender inequality between Sweden and the United Kingdom are noteworthy. It is apparent that not only does Sweden have more women already in leadership and board positions, but Sweden also has a much larger pool of female talent in middle management positions and therefore a higher proportion of future leaders who are women.

This substantial difference between the United Kingdom and Sweden has strong and obvious links with gender equality in parenting. Any researcher will tell you that we can't claim causality by simply looking at these data. However, according to UNICEF, family friendly policies that were introduced in the Scandinavian countries in the last 50 years have both increased female employment rates and increased GDP per capita by 10–20%.[44]

To understand more, we need to interview women. I did exactly that and my findings show that there is a causal link between how women are treated with regards to pregnancy, maternity leave and beyond, and their likelihood to stay and succeed in their careers. Men taking parental leave produces more women in leadership. However, although Sweden is statistically much more gender equal than, say, the United Kingdom, the country is still far from offering full gender equality. The work there continues, both at home and in the boardroom. Just as men need to make space for women in finance and business, women need to make space for men at home. Mothers need to let go of some of their parenting control. This fulcrum means that gender equality will not be achieved by simply requesting men to change. Everyone, regardless of their gender or position, needs to contribute, and bear in mind that everyone will also reap the benefits.

Systemic parenting bias

A major problem in the drive towards equality for mothers is that in countries where shared parental leave is not properly supported, much of the maternity pay is borne by employers. In most countries, there is little contribution from the state. This means that employers are biased already at the interview stage, before they have even employed a woman who might one day become pregnant. It is difficult for a small company to afford paying for maternity leave and to fill her absence with an interim recruit. The company also knows that it is usually the mother who will rush home if a child is unwell, if the school calls or if something else happens. A male candidate offers no such potential hidden expense.

Why doesn't the father do it?

Well, he could in theory. There's no reason why not. But by not having taken time off with the baby in the early days, he is not accustomed to taking a lead parental role and therefore is not expected to do so by others either.

Contrast this with countries where shared parental leave is established, and where pay for that leave is borne by the state. Employers (and therefore potential employees) do not have the same problems at the interview stage. They know that nearly a third of fathers are as likely to be at home with their baby as mothers. Shared parental leave means that fathers become used to parenting and a natural contact for childcare providers and schools. As a result, they are then more likely to rush home to attend to the child when needed – giving the mother more time to focus on work.

If society allows and expects the father and mother to share parenting equally the situation in the workplace is different. In an interview setting, the employer is then faced with two people applying for the role, instead of a (potential) mother and a man without any such (negative) prospects.

Shared parental leave was finally introduced in the United Kingdom in 2015 – some 41 years after Sweden. I hope that in 41 years we will look back at this and think that fathers not being allowed to be at home with their children, is as ridiculous as women not being allowed to open bank accounts in their own names until the 1970s.

Despite the logical benefits of shared parental leave, encouraging fathers to take the time off is complicated. One of the reasons for this is pay. With fathers usually earning more than mothers, it is not economically viable for most families that fathers are only paid statutory rates when on leave. It remains cheaper for the person who earns less to take time off so we need to tackle policy making and gender pay inequality simultaneously.

Support and sacrifice

As part of my current research, I am investigating the support systems that surround men and women who make it to senior positions in financial services, along with the sacrifices they have to make to get there. This is important because, traditionally, men who are successful in the industry, have stay-at-home wives or wives who work part time who take on the responsibility for childcare and logistics in the home, thus allowing their husbands to focus fully on their careers. These men may not, in the midst of their careers, feel that giving up time with their children and families is a sacrifice. This is because historically and culturally men have not and still are not assumed to be consistently present in the family, to, for example: collect children from school, accompany children to medical and dental appointments, organise birthday parties, cook dinner and arrange the logistics of their children's daily lives. However, for women, on average, not being present is experienced as having to sacrifice something that is really important in life. This leads to women feeling guilty and as though they are not enough at work or at home. Another conundrum for women in leadership positions is that they are faced with 'trying to do it all'. Women expect themselves to be fully present both at home and at work and they do not want to give up experiencing their children growing up. The sacrifices that women have to make to prioritise their careers are therefore often perceived to be bigger than those men face, regardless of whether a woman is a mother or has sacrificed having children for her career. The perception of others around these women is also confused because they expect mothers to take the lead role in parenting. Or they expect women to have children, so those women who do not are often left misunderstood or pitied. Researchers show how women report having to make substantial personal and family sacrifices to achieve career success,[45] to a greater extent than men,[46] views that were echoed in the interviews I conducted. Many women feel that they need to sacrifice either their careers, or having children or seeing their children grow up. The playing field is not level between men who have support at home and women who still devote significant time and efforts at home. She has less time than her male colleagues, making the competition field uneven.

However, like mothers, fathers worry about the economic impact of taking time off with their children. Families tend to make an economically motivated and culturally expected decision rather than one which is based on that which may be best for all the participants in the family. Whilst women now have most of the legal rights they need to fully participate in the financial system in many countries, fathers have the legal rights they need to fully participate in parenting in only a very few countries. For fathers to have equal parenting rights to mothers is a rarity. The consideration towards both parents sharing parental leave is growing but legal reform is slow. Only a small percentage of the organisations that can afford it, including a few of the large banks, have adopted policies that allow fathers to take paid parental leave and actually encourage them to do so. This work is incredibly important, but fathers find stepping forward to take leave quite frightening because of what others may think. Interviews with male role models who have taken time off evidence this. But these interviews also reveal how incredibly rewarding the time off is, not only for bonding with their children, but also for understanding, respecting and supporting their partners, that is, creating a mutual understanding. Fathers who did not or were not able to take time off feel more excluded from life at home, and from the experience of seeing their children grow up. This contributes to an increasing gap in understanding between the partners. More debate is required around a father's rights to parent, with research addressing legal reforms as well as the gender bias and stereotyping attached to fathers who choose to parent. We also need to acknowledge the loss and the grief that many fathers feel they have to supress.

Gender equality and the bridge to intersectional practices

Progress for Women is progress for everyone.

(Catalyst, 2017)[47]

Equality for women means progress for all.

(United Nations, 2014)[48]

The positive impact of gender equality in financial services has far reaching effects on intersectional practices, family life and society as a whole. This is evident in many of the statistics cited in relation to female performance in Chapter 5. Women are more inclusive leaders who value diversity. Therefore, increasing the proportion of 'normal' non alpha women in leadership positions in financial services will improve diversity and inclusion within organisations. Both in relation to employees and consumers because women are more likely than men to listen to the unusual voice around the table.

Together with colleagues, I established the Economic Equality Impact Group (EEIG) at King's Business School.[49] The EEIG focuses on gender *and* the wider diversity and inclusion agendas in the financial services industry. The EEIG is needed because, despite how inclusive practices are a key strategic priority, evidence suggests that people, organisations and even governments still tend to work in silos, that is, in isolation from each other. The collaborative approach is the essence of diversity, inclusion and equality.

What became apparent in the initial start-up phase of the EEIG was how much the contributors wanted to focus not only on gender but also on wider diversity and inclusion. This speaks volumes and supports our argument that improved gender diversity can contribute to improved intersectionality in the industry. However, without the support of government policies and corporate policies, it will be very difficult to create long-lasting positive impact. In Sweden, I am the co-creator of the Swedish Community for Sustainable Finance at the University of Gothenburg.[50] Our group focuses on the potential for the financial services sector to be a fundamental vehicle to develop and promote sustainable practices and to act as a role model for other business areas. With its powerful reach and interactions with all areas of society, the impact of increased sustainable practices in the industry can advance practices in other domains.

Equality for women in financial services can contribute to increased equality for all. Sustainable practices in financial services can contribute to sustainable practices in other sectors.

Notes

1 Inman (2018).
2 USA News (2021).
3 Fackförbund (2021).
4 Försäkringskassan (2021a).
5 Gov.UK (2021a); Striking Women (2021).

6 Petter (2019).
7 Citizens Advice (2021).
8 The Money Advice Service (2021a).
9 The Money Advice Service (2021b).
10 Gov.UK (2021b).
11 The Money Advice Service (2021c).
12 Avanza (2020); Försäkringskassan (2021b).
13 Försäkringskassan (2021c).
14 The Conversation (2018).
15 Lambert (2008).
16 Gov.UK (2021c).
17 On Average (2021)
18 Göteborgs Stad (2021).
19 Brown Calder (2018).
20 Connelly and Kimmel (2003).
21 DW (2021).
22 UN News (2021).
23 European Commission (2021).
24 The World Bank Group (2021).
25 World Health Organization (2019).
26 Catalyst (2020b).
27 World Health Organization (2019).
28 Windsor et al. (2020).
29 Fitch Ratings (2021); Smith (2021).
30 The Economist (2021).
31 Moise (2021).
32 JP Morgan Chase (2021).
33 Moise & Morris (2021).
34 Velati (2021).
35 Moise & Morris (2021).
36 Moise & Morris (2021).
37 UK Parliament (2021b).
38 Ekonomifakta (2021a).
39 Ekonomifakta (2021b).
40 Chef (2020).
41 Catalyst (2020c).
42 Ekonomifakta (2021c).
43 Goodley (2020).
44 Unicef (2021).
45 Walsh (2012).
46 Groysberg and Abrahams (2014).
47 Catalyst (2017).
48 UN News (2014).
49 The Economic Equality Impact Group (2021).
50 Swedish Community for Sustainable Finance (2021).

7

ACTIONS TO REDUCE GENDER BIAS AND INCREASE GENDER EQUALITY

In this book, I have demonstrated how gender attitudes and behaviour are to a large extent manufactured by society. This extends to participants in the financial services industry and within the family. Negative gender bias puts limitations on women's potential to the detriment of women's employment and retirement income. It restrains potential economic output. The COVID-19 pandemic exacerbated gender inequality, with negative effects disproportionately affecting women. The strategies that firms choose to 'return to normal' after the pandemic will be crucial for women in particular, because they have more to lose. Negative gender bias is particularly acute in the financial services industry and it is especially pivotal to address negative bias here because of its standing as the world's most powerful industry: It is an industry that underpins all activity in society, has the highest financial rewards for employees and also the highest gender pay inequality. The financial services industry has the potential to lead the way; to role model gender equal practices and showcase how increased diversity and equality will improve lives and profits for everyone. With a forward looking and inclusive approach, it could become an admired industry that is the natural choice for diverse employees and consumers. To make this happen the industry needs to break free from homogeneity and group thinking, enable equal opportunities for all and embrace diverse leadership. Financial services needs to stop being afraid of difference. I accept that it is difficult to remove gender simply or quickly from the financial services industry because it is so entrenched in its culture, language, architecture and history. But if the industry and our societies are to thrive in the future these changes are not optional. Instead of trying to make people more like the industry, the industry needs to become more like the people, in all their diverse manifestations.

DOI: 10.4324/9781003198109-7

In this chapter, we will look at some simple and effective actions that the financial services industry, policy makers, families employees, consumers of all genders can undertake to enable and expedite more gender equal practices that will benefit everyone. As a society and as an industry we jointly created gender based associations. We can now use the steps in this chapter to reinvent gender biased attitudes and behaviour in financial services. This will also future proof the industry and unlock the full gender potential for female employees and consumers.

Things the industry can and should address

Focus on transformational leadership

There is an urgent need to increase diversity in leadership positions. Diverse teams are too rare in financial services. Organisations need to transform their leadership structures to enable leaders to challenge practices. They need the courage to recruit and promote diverse team members and to hear and value the unusual voices. Rewards will be reaped through improved performance, client acquisition and happier employees. Research shows how leaders can both proactively influence and reactively encourage team diversity.[1] Successful leaders who are proficient in managing diversity need cognitive understanding, social perceptiveness and behavioural flexibility. It is more difficult to lead diverse teams but the skills of female leaders are perfect for the future transformational leader. Women's inclusive and collaborative leadership practices increase intersectionality, facilitate the performance of diverse teams and thus help to future-proof organisations. On the contrary, homogeneous leadership blocks the performance of diverse teams. Leaders, regardless of their gender or background need support to develop the right skills to be transformational. Therefore, organisations need to invest in excellent executive education, education which focuses on diverse practices and intersectionality.

Use the transformational leaders already in the talent pool

The phrase 'there isn't a sufficient pool of women' to promote to senior leadership positions is becoming rather tired. The talent pool could have been built several times over given the number of years the phrase has been around. Managers need to listen to their employees. Many women feel that their only option is to leave the industry once they become mothers as they are otherwise faced with discrimination in the workplace at the same time as they are not able to be around to see their children grow up. The promotion doors are firmly shut, and flexibility can be frowned upon and considered a weakness. Be empathetic of mothers who usually carry the heavier burden at home. Offer them the flexibility they need, and they will remain loyal and supportive.

These women are a pipeline to the future. Once they leave the industry, they disappear from the talent pool. If they return, they often do so to different, more junior and flexible positions perhaps in a completely different industry. Make changes in the organisation so that mothers and carers can continue to contribute and do not need to feel guilty about having increased responsibilities at home. Their children form part of the future talent pool. The problem is not that the women leave, the problem is that the industry makes it hard for women to stay.

Update the language, culture and architecture of financial services

The gender of finance and investing is firmly alpha male. It was created by men for men and its language and culture have proved resistant to change. We use words like 'aggressive', 'generate alpha', 'bull and bear market' – words that do not appeal to most people regardless of their gender.

The industry tends to overcomplicate documentation, using incomprehensible terminology and acronyms that are understood only by a small homogeneous group of people.

Its buildings can be phallic symbols and the equipment within them is designed to work for men, not women.

The easiest (and least expensive) action is to address the language and look and feel of documentation and materials.

Gather a diverse team of people to compose a list of outdated language that the organisation uses in internal and external written material as well as video and voice productions. Recreate the language to appeal to a diverse audience drawing on the feedback from the diverse team. I discuss this very topic in my article 'Time for the financial industry to jettison the jargon' published by Professional Wealth Management[2] in which I argue that we should not need a dictionary to understand how our pensions work. This is one rapid and effective change that will ensure that the industry has a wide appeal and feels inclusive.

Next time the firm redecorates, updates equipment, rebrands or moves offices, think about what works best for a diverse team. For example, what type of computer equipment, desks, meeting rooms, lift system, coffee machines, colours and temperature – the list goes on – appeal to the target employee and customer base. These are stakeholders that will help grow the business in the future. The strategy needs to be forward looking instead of clinging onto archaic practices that need to become extinct.

Ensure psychological safety

For many of the people with the skills we really need, starting a career in financial services is a scary prospect. It is not a warm and friendly culture that feels welcoming, more like one that needs to be conquered. Integrating compassion and empathy in organisations will not only make them attractive to diverse employees. It will also facilitate innovation and reduce risk because everyone is able to speak up. We need a corporate culture that feels psychologically safe and truly supportive of diversity.

Tackle embedded diverse beliefs and practices

Just because organisations have policies in place, it doesn't mean they are 'lived' or embedded throughout the organisation. The same goes for regulatory support. Its mere existence without gender diverse practices being embedded in society makes it ineffectual. There needs to be a genuine belief in gender diversity both within organisations and the societies within which they operate for them to work. This is demonstrated in a 2019 study of over 1,000 large companies across a range of industries in 35 countries. The study reports that gender diversity only relates to higher rates of production when gender diversity is seen as *normative*,[3] i.e., is established and embedded in the firm culture, firm practices and the country of operation. Organisations must implement gender diverse policies, believe in them and ensure they are adhered to. These need to be values that are shared by *everyone* who works in the organisation, rather than simply being just a box ticking or quota exercise. Its leadership needs to do more than simply say they believe in gender equality. Instead, they must role model how they will no longer tolerate inequality, they celebrate positive behaviour and improve unhelpful practices. They need to measure the impact of their policies and demonstrate the outcomes in their organisations. It is not a top down approach, it is a throughout the organisation approach. Diverse leadership and inclusive work practices become the new culture where all stakeholders with power actually believe in and articulate diversity. The leadership teams need to role model gender diverse practices and penalise exclusionary behaviour.

Update professional development

Unconscious bias training has increased in popularity in recent years. To be effective, the training needs to be tailored to the needs of the specific organisation and provide solutions that can be implemented in the day to day work. This challenges organisations to take an active and involved approach to developing and delivering training rather than adopting a tick-box approach. General psychological concepts can be difficult to translate to workable solutions and the learning may be limited if organisations are not consciously aware of the outcomes they need. Furthermore, the success of these outcomes need to be measured so they don't fall flat and to ensure momentum is not lost.

Work on role modelling and reverse messaging

Being a trailblazer is hard work. It is much easier to strive towards promotion into a position previously held by someone who looks like us or comes from a similar background. The trailblazing trait is generally associated with the risk-taking behaviour of alpha females or alpha males and is not inclusive. Applying for a position that has previously been occupied by someone who looks like you, is more achievable both for the promoting manager and the prospective candidate Therein lies a potential danger. For organisations that do not already have a diverse team of leaders, it is important that the leaders let employees know that anyone in the organisation can achieve those roles regardless of their backgrounds. Reverse messaging can successfully challenge stereotypes. Organisations need to present women as the successful leaders that they are and can be, instead of portraying them as unstable and lucky to be promoted. Seeing just diverse leaders instead of just diverse side characters will encourage others to apply. We naturally associate male leaders with authority and power. Through reverse messaging organisations can extend this association to female leaders.

In 2021, two female role models, Isabel Schnabel, executive board member of the European Central Bank and Margarita Delgado, deputy governor of the Bank of Spain, expressed the need for central banks to devise strategies to recruit and promote more women. They emphasised the need to have a *strategy* because without decisive action change will not happen. These strategies may include some positive discrimination to address the gender imbalance and hidden barriers to women's progressions.[4] Today, there is still a sense that we need to be apologetic about such actions.

Look at recruitment with fresh, enlightened eyes

Hiring and promotion criteria are indirectly male skewed, skewed because hiring managers are biased to look for people who will 'fit in the team'. Instead hire those who do not fit in the team, those who stand out and will challenge the existing team. Look for heterogeneity instead of homogeneity so that new team members add complementary skills, bring diversity of thought and the ability to induce innovative business practices. If the organisation is able to see and hear these employees, future clients will feel seen and heard. Access to the financial services industry is harder the further you move away from the archetype: the white, middle class male. This is true for both employees and consumers.

Value the skills that the industry needs

Financial services firms continue to value traditional alpha male skills that are perceived to be, but are actually not, that essential or useful. The skills that women bring are exactly those that the industry needs. These skills include relationship management and the ability to connect emotionally with other people, which are absolutely key for being successful in business. Banks pay to develop these skills among their employees (through continuing professional development courses) and yet the skills themselves are not as valued as they should be. The stronger the relationships you have with everyone you interact with at work the more successful you will be. Women are world leaders in relationship management and connection. These skills may be undervalued but they are essential for business success. Organisations need to value them and cease celebrating overconfidence which is so detrimental for performance and risk taking. The culture in financial services means that there is too much focus on quantitative skills, the exact skills that women have been conditioned to feel less confident about but which are much easier to learn than emotional intelligence. So put together a diverse team of people to rewrite job specifications and performance evaluation criteria. Think about what skills people really need to be successful. 'Excellent financial modelling skills' may remain important but 'The ability to build trusting relationships' may be more important, as are 'Active listening, empathy and collaboration skills'. Ensure that management and everyone in the organisation value these skills as much as they do the easily measurable 'olden days' skills set.

Embrace flexible working

Many people regardless of their gender/carer/parent status were not granted proper flexibility to work from home until it was demanded by governments. The evidence is that these practices work, with the financial services industry in particular continuing to thrive during the 2020/2021 lockdowns. It may be tempting to try to turn the clock back: discuss strategy on the golf course, conclude deals in fancy restaurants, and invite clients on all expenses paid trips and experiences to win their business. These strategies will again exclude those who need to rush home to look after children or other domestic duties or simply want to do something else in their spare time. Organisations must consider not just offering flexible working practices but instead *requiring* them from their staff so that everyone is offered fair and equal opportunities. This will also benefit families whose children will see more of their parents and organisations whose staff are less likely to burn out from too long and unsociable working hours and exhausting commutes. Make flexible working a contractual obligation.

At the time of writing, the responses by organisations to the potential to change working practices positively following the pandemic vary greatly by industry and jurisdiction. Senior leadership needs to role model inclusive decision making about what best practice for their organisation should be. In my experience and the experience of many others in the industry, clients actually embrace flexibility. The culture of 'jacket on the back of the chair' plus 24/7 availability of employees (especially those looking for promotion) are not justifiable practices.

On diversity and difference

Measure the diversity impact

The financial services industry thrives on and thinks in numbers but surprisingly, to my knowledge, no one has yet developed a tool that computes a profit and loss statement linked to gender equality measures or even linked to the performance and cost of female and male employees. Researchers and business school students are becoming increasingly interested in analysing the impact of ESG (environmental, social and governance) strategies. Arguably diversity and inclusion and more specifically gender diverse measures form part of the S for 'social' in ESG. As ESG reporting becomes a regulatory requirement for financial services in Europe and elsewhere, measurement of diversity and inclusion become more important. Organisations need to develop an internal gender audit tool to evidence how successful or not their current and evolving strategies around gender are. This tool needs to include revenues generated by and the costs associated with employees and teams run by diverse genders. The audit can be used in strategy conversations and to inform practices and policies both relating to employees and clients. This is also at the heart of good corporate finance practice. It focuses not only on shareholders but also on all the stakeholders of the business. Most corporate strategic priorities about gender equality are voluntary, not backed up by regulatory requirements. For example, in the United Kingdom, companies with 250 or more staff must *report* their gender pay gap (paused in 2020 and 2021 due to the pandemic), but there is no requirement to *close* the gap. The same is true for female representation on boards or in senior leadership positions in most countries. Banks admit to being poor at reviewing their progress in the diversity space. Joining up all these initiatives and addressing them holistically will make a big difference. After we have measured the effectiveness of corporate policies we need to take what we learned to improve them to create actionable targeted policies in the workplace. And we will judge them on their real long-lasting positive impacts on reducing inequality and increasing diversity. The market will then do its judging as well. But there is also a need to create an evidence base where we measure the efforts that go into the strategic priorities and the results that they deliver. Otherwise, the policies are merely tokenistic or may not have the intended impact and therefore need redesigning. The industry thinks in numbers, let's show it how profitable increased diversity can be.

Celebrate difference

Organisations don't have to be afraid of difference and diversity. Remember how it is the combination of a diverse range of assets in a portfolio that produces the highest return at a given level of risk. That is also the right business strategy. Dare to move away from homogeneous group thinking. We often talk about women being afraid of taking risks by doing unfamiliar things. That limits women's career and portfolio performance potential. This is an example of an entire industry shying away from taking risks, behaviour that limits the industry's performance. Not being courageous enough to embrace difference and diversity is the real risk that the industry is facing.

Showcase diversity

Demonstrate diverse practices to clients. Look at the current and future client base. Mirror that in the organisation because that is what organisations need to look like. Consider the skills and traits that clients are looking for: those are the skills that are needed in organisations. If the business does not mirror the diversity of its existing and prospective target market, address this in recruitment and retention processes. This is important for clients to make the organisation their natural choice instead of feeling intimidated or patronised by it. Until the balance has been addressed, implement strategies that show that the organisation understands diversity. Then look at the consumers of financial services because they are the future clients. They consist of the entire population of people living where the business operates.

Address the client focus

Have the client in focus when planning business strategy. What business models work for the business and its clients? Do clients enjoy the alpha language, culture and architecture? Some firms try to adopt models that do not require constant travel and realise that their clients really don't mind if their banker has children that they want to spend time with. Good companies ought to recognise the additional effort it takes for a woman to reach the same position as a man and try to make it easier for those who follow. Some do this through offering mentorship opportunities to women leaders, or sponsorship for young women to join financial services firms. It is also important to arrange seminars for women in finance, seminars that address the perceived lower levels of knowledge and confidence among female employees and consumers. Clients are human beings who enjoy dealing with other human beings who just like themselves sometimes find life a struggle. They are not all power dressing.

On families

Decide whether or not we want people to have children

Governments have to carry the main financial burden of parental leave and childcare. Otherwise organisations will remain biased against mothers. We need a policy that works for *everyone*: fathers, mothers, children and society. Most current policies do not work for *anyone*. Inclusive policy making will also challenge the stereotype that men are not good carers. Just like women were never given the opportunities in business that they deserve, men were never given the opportunities to care for their children. If you are a policy maker, create policies that support both fathers and mothers (or mothers and mothers or fathers and fathers — whatever the parental configuration looks like) to parent together. We need to fix the things that for generations have contributed to the development of inequalities for women and for men. It is impossible to really tackle gender inequality unless we have full *societal* support via positive changes in policy. The current parent (maternity) leave provisions in most countries are still stuck in the past. The regulations at the moment still support the archetypical old school system of parenting, in which the mother is assumed to take on parental responsibility and the father is responsible for bringing in the money.

Stop calling it maternity leave

A child has (in most cases) got two parents. The parents can be same sex or not. Every parent ought to have the right to parent their child. The term 'maternity leave' is discriminatory, it discriminates against fathers and mothers alike. In 2021, I invited senior business leaders from the United Kingdom and Sweden to discuss parental leave practices and their impact on perceptions and abilities for parents to progress in their careers. It became immediately evident that the shared parental leave practices introduced in Sweden in 1974 and the subsequent investment into removing the gender of parental leave have contributed to normalising the notion that anyone who is a parent can take time off to parent their child, regardless of gender or background. This has contributed to more women in leadership and therefore also challenged the male gender of leadership. Sweden still has a long way to go but other countries have much further to travel.

Celebrate parenting and caring, celebrate non-parenting

Managers need to facilitate their employees to be guilt-free parents and carers. No one in financial services should need to choose between their careers and being a parent. The pandemic has proved that both are possible. Although mothers bore the brunt of the parenting and household (unpaid) work, fathers also increased the time they spent looking after their children. That was good for fathers, good for children and good for families. The industry continued to thrive. It now has to continue to ensure that it is socially acceptable for fathers to parent their children and to share parenting responsibilities. It needs to remove the bias a woman of a childbearing age or a woman with children faces during interviews. The attitudes of the current and future client base can also be taken into account. They are also parents and carers, and they will place importance on those values being present in organisations. Organisations also need to tackle outdated perceptions about women who are not, for whatever reason, mothers. These women are often left to pick up the pieces and cover holiday periods that parents tend to want to take off. This was also apparent during the pandemic when those who lived alone or did not have carer roles had more time to work. But because someone has more time to work doesn't mean they should or even want to.

Take parental leave

Allowing women to progress more at work can also be a powerful liberation for men. Allowing fathers to parent more will create better balanced families and more equality in personal relationships and a higher level of satisfaction for men. The world then benefits from future generations in which all genders become accustomed to both parents parenting and both parents being able to have careers. Everyone wins, and the world wins with them. If you are a father, you must take parental leave. Role model that parenting is for both parents to enjoy and don't become the man who regrets not spending time with his children. I have not yet met a father in his 50s or 60s who wished he had spent more time working, but I have met many who regret not having spent more time with their children.

On women, for women and about women

Invest in her, understand her

Be mindful of a woman's journey to get to where she is and be aware of what you bring into the room with her - regardless of whether she is a client or an employee. You are the person who can make a difference to her. This is an important responsibility. Show her that you really care about that, that you care about her and her future. Women do not want fluff. Client initiatives targeted towards women clients have failed in many banks over the years. Women can feel patronised when offered 'pink' solutions or 'women friendly' investments. Instead beware of homogeneous group thinking. Finance professionals find it easier to do business with those who are similar. Diversity is more difficult to understand. But the rewards are high when you earn the trust of a woman or another underserved section of society, because they are much more likely to be loyal, and to recommend you to others.

Reassess risk taking

The biggest risk women face is not taking risks. They have to dare themselves to become role models for other women and other underrepresented groups of people, to invest in their careers or personal portfolios. Reframe what risk means and understand it properly. Demystify risk for clients. Be aware of the difference between risk capacity and risk tolerance. While risk tolerance is a self-expressed wish to adopt risk, capacity is linked to the financial situation and how much risk is affordable. We need to educate underinvested clients about investing, increase their confidence and make them aware that the real risk is not investing, and not securing their financial futures. To do this we might need to reframe risk, to put risk in context. This is because risk means different things to different people. Researchers often adopt this approach when asking for people's opinions.

Reassess confidence

Forget about confidence. No one is completely certain about their actions, some who appear very confident are just better at hiding their uncertainty. Rely on your knowledge and preparation, you are there because of your skills, your contribution and your potential. At the same time the industry must stop thinking that overconfidence is the same as competence and instead consider the skills that their employees bring.

Consider nudges

We still need to give women specific nudges and tips to motivate them to apply for roles in financial services, and then about how to manage their careers. It is harder on a scale depending on their background. For example, being a privately educated white, straight woman is much easier than being a non-straight woman of colour. There is still a serious lack of acceptance of difference, and still a need for gender specific advice on how to succeed. Women who have made it in financial services, who have become role models are best placed to advise others. So if and when you have made, it share your expertise.

Walk in her shoes

Empathy is a skill often associated with psychotherapists. But it is also an important skill for finance professionals. Clients bring their financial anxieties to you, and you need to support them. You are not expected to know everything about your clients, where they are from or their negative and positive life experiences. But you can be curious about them and empathise with them. A woman of colour will have had to work much harder to get to where she is, especially compared to a white man. Acknowledge this and empathise with her journey. Be proud of her and she will feel that you genuinely care.

Trust in relationships

Trust is particularly important in the financial services industry, an industry that people quite understandably find difficult to trust. Gender differences in confidence and risk tolerance are much greater in male dominated domains. How we treat women as investment clients is therefore very important, and the ability for advisors to enable trust in their relationships with women clients is critical for how much they will invest and how much they will dare to borrow.

Mind the life expectancy gap

Taking responsibility to ensure that we have enough money to fund our retirement is very important. This is particularly important as women live longer than men. For example, as women in Europe live on average 5 years longer than men,[5] they need 5 years additional retirement income and a larger retirement savings pot compared to men. Communicate to female clients that not investing is the real risk.

Remember: women are not born less confident, knowledgeable or risk intolerant

These gender based assumptions were created by society. We created differences between women and men that are not necessarily 'biological' and 'natural' but which have resulted in gender stereotypes and gender bias. These are (often negative and limiting) beliefs that we hold about people because of their gender and they affect our behaviour. Just like we created them, we have the power to undo them. Don't allow their or your own gender to interfere. Lower your gender based assumptions and raise your expectations. See the person in front of you for who they are without placing gender based limitations on them.

Notes

1 Homan et al. (2020).
2 Baeckström (2021a)
3 Turban et al. (2019).
4 Arnold and Dombey (2021).
5 Eurostat (2019b).

8

CONCLUSION

The win-win of taking gender out of financial services

We need to ask ourselves what a financial services industry built by an intersectionally diverse team of people would look like. A team that is made up of women, men and people of other diverse genders and people from different backgrounds. People who represent marginalised communities relating to, e.g., race, religion and lesbian, gay, bisexual or transgender – groups of people for whom the inequality gap is the biggest and whose voices have been heard the least. The people who were not involved in the original design.

Instead of plastering over cracks, redesigning the financial services industry should become a powerful and continuously compelling proposal. A cleverly composed environmental, social and governance strategy in financial services would consider how the industry can be rebuilt to harness the resources of all its contributors for the benefit of all. This future industry will operate in harmony with society instead of benefiting a few but being destructive or restrictive to many. Gender equality is an excellent starting point. The financial services industry is the ideal place to start because of its power, profitability and its substantially larger inequalities relative to other industries.

Gender equality in financial services has always been important but it has become more urgent as a result of the COVID-19 pandemic. Urgent because during the pandemic we witnessed how fragile progress has been and how quickly positive developments became undone. In some areas, 40 years of gender equality progress was wiped away in a stroke. This demonstrates how gender diversity is not yet a stable part of our economic thinking.

> Never forget that it only takes a political, economic or religious crisis for women's rights to be called into question. These rights can never be taken for granted. You must remain vigilant throughout your life.
>
> *(Simone de Beauvoir, 1949)[1]*

DOI: 10.4324/9781003198109-8

Finance rules the world and finance is currently ruled by men. We are hoping that these men can now see at least the business opportunity that is brought about by diversity and equality. But if we carry on at this pace it will take over 200 years before women are equal to men in the labour force. It is obvious that money invested wisely has the power to transform businesses and families and whole countries. But a financial services industry that is institutionally gender biased can never claim to be investing money wisely or even investing in the diversified portfolios it recommends to its clients.

Women are deterred from applying for jobs in alpha male domains but it's the alpha-male domains that need female skills the most. Large banks are investing in trying to attract more female talent through women focused recruitment and retention initiatives. But a big part of the problem is that financial institutions are trying to get women to become more like them, to adopt their male gender.

Women can survive without having a career in the financial services industry, but the financial services industry cannot thrive without women. We can't afford not to change.

If finance, instead of being created by alpha men for alpha men, had been created by women, what would it look like today? If it had been created by a diverse team of members of society, what would it look like? Who would have been the beneficiaries of a diversely designed financial services industry? I believe that it is most likely the benefits would, perhaps for the first time, trickle down to many more participants in society. And that resources and opportunities will be shared more equally, not just within a small and mainly homogeneous group of people.

As a society we created the negative and limiting gender stereotypes, and so we have the power to disentangle gender and recreate our attitudes and behaviour. Because gender is elastic. To enable real change, we need to recreate gender in finance *and* parenting. Women are good at business and good for business and men are good for children and good parents. All we need to do to achieve this is to stop putting limitations on ourselves or others because of gender. But because biases are often unconscious and sometimes difficult to identify, this presents a challenge for managers, who are not usually educated in psychology or gender, but are left with the difficult task of detecting the layers of disadvantage, stereotypes and biases within their organisations. The task is bigger than them and it isn't fair or sensible to expect individuals to achieve this change on their own. We need organisations and governments to adopt policies that minimise bias, policies that form the basis for gender equal practices.

One of the reasons for the fragility of gender equality progress is that it has become customary to frame gender diversity as a problem that needs fixing rather than as the opportunity it is to unlock the full potential of people regardless of what gender they associate themselves with, bringing benefits for all. Because of the domination of the financial services industry, gender equality practices within it represent an excellent starting point towards a full potential world in which we are all able to contribute to the best of our abilities instead of our contributions being limited by our backgrounds and our gender. We therefore need a financial service industry that is truly diverse and inclusive. An industry that looks after all its diverse customers to offer them the services that they want to pay for. An industry that offers all its employees equal opportunities to succeed regardless of their gender or diverse background. Gender equality will make the industry more successful and will contribute to more balanced relationships and healthier families. This will translate into a positive contribution to GDP. It really is a win–win.

The economic shock caused by COVID-19 presents a chance to reset and bring about change. A chance to ditch archaic practices and future proof the industry. Despite how women bore the brunt of domestic and childcare duties, so being forced to manage an increased workload alongside their careers, the pandemic also provided new opportunities, largely through ways of working that didn't exist before. The opportunity for mothers to pitch business to global customers from their home working spaces instead of needing to leave their children to go on lengthy business trips, is just one example. But the pandemic also came with an increased domestic workload so this is far from sustainable as it stands. If not managed well, the pandemic presents the risk that practices revert quickly and the momentum for change lost. It is up to the senior leaders in financial services to decide the strategy that they wish to adopt. Currently, with the divergence in strategies across institution and countries, there is no consensus for the best working practices for the industry. This creates instability and uncertainty which makes it easier for organisations to revert to homogeneous group thinking practices.

Just as gender based attitudes and behaviour are fluid and elastic, so is the financial services industry. We have witnessed positive change. We now need more of it and faster, only then it will be stable enough to withstand external shocks and crises.

The process for getting there will be faster and simpler if we reframe gender inclusion as one of opportunities and benefits, rather than viewing it as a problem. Not doing so means that gender equality policies will remain tick box exercises rather than becoming embedded and stable practices that generate economic gain and withstand crises.

We need to *keep our eyes on the prize:*

Prizes include the economic and societal win–win of a gender equal financial services industry. We need to acknowledge and celebrate the trailblazing women who have worked their way to the top in the industry, positions that no women before have ever held, for example, Maggie Lena Walker. But let's also showcase and celebrate female role models who continue to work in the industry at various seniority levels, women who are single, married, mothers, carers. All these women pave the way for others regardless of their gender or background to envisage a career in financial services. We also need to really understand the women of the pandemic. These are the women who despite increased pressure and workload at home, continued their work, and didn't give up, regardless of increased inequality in the industry, the home and society as a whole.

It's also important that we don't forget the men. We need to celebrate all the men who support women. The male managers, partners, fathers, friends and brothers who invest in and believe in women. The men without whose support gender equality is not possible. The men who role model that someone doesn't have to look like or be like them, to be inspirational and successful in financial services. The men who mentor progress for those around them. We cannot achieve our goal of a gender equal financial services industry without men like these.

The prizes we have fixed our eyes on are for everyone. It's not a new notion, but it's a true one: together, we are better than the sum of our parts. Considering that women already outperform our negative expectations, one can only imagine what would happen if women were given a genuinely equal opportunity to succeed.

Gender equality is fractal and forces us to look at other inequalities. I have discussed how a black woman banker from 1903 is still a lesson for us all today. Women know what it is like to have to work their way up from a disadvantaged position predisposing them to become the inclusive leaders evident in the collaborative traits of female leaders. Increased gender equality leads to more diverse opinions valued around the table. My white woman history does not equip me to report on other stories but research by me and others lead me to believe strongly that all the changes that move us towards gender equality can also play a positive part in helping us to address other structural inequities. Change begins with each of us – I am one woman, writing this book and dedicating my career to improve equality in the financial services industry, creating the Economic Equality Impact Group at King's Business School in 2020 and the Swedish Community for Sustainable Finance at the University of Gothenburg in 2021. In my groups, I ensure that the research agenda is established through discussion in diverse groups. This is an inclusive practice but as team intelligence increases with diversity, it is also a clever strategy. The only strategy that makes sense regardless of the industry.

No one's gender should determine what contribution they can make to the world. We need to allow everyone to be the best that they can be and to have access to the opportunities that they require to succeed. All of us need to start thinking like this. Together we need to do what we can to remove gender from the financial services industry. This may be a long journey because the way the industry is, and how we feel and behave, have been built up not only during our lifetime but also throughout the generations that came before. Our internalised beliefs about gender have become important components of our unconscious minds and we have created a collective unconscious understanding about gender in financial services. It is often difficult to fully understand culture or its origins. But change also has long-lasting positive effects and impact. The cultural belief that males make better leaders than women needs to be challenged. Continued reverse messaging, role modelling and investing in female leaders can shift these internalised beliefs. Organisations need to learn their unconscious patterns of culture and gender beliefs. An organisation can't expect to change its gender patterns of behaviour until it understands *why* it has the values it has and *how* those were developed.

If you read this and you are a policy maker, you need to ensure that the right policies are in place in our society. If you read this and you are an organisation, you need to make sure that you have the right policies, that you believe in those policies and that you invest in developing all your staff. If you read this and you are an individual, you need to invest in yourself and others around you regardless of gender. Only by working together can we unlock our real potential in society, in business and as individuals.

Nobody needs to become a stereotypically alpha male or alpha female to be successful in finance. After all, many of the current and to an increasing extent, the future consumers of financial services are most definitely not made up of alpha men and/or superwomen. Women need to be assured that it is not women who need to change. It is the financial services industry that needs to adapt to women. To become inclusive towards women as well as men, and female facing as well as male facing.

Perhaps one of the reasons that we have more than one gender is because we are better together. Problems in a good relationship are halved when shared. Solutions are found in empathy. Business is also about relationships. Business problems are also halved when shared, solutions are found and money is made. Everyone stands to gain from supporting each other. People supporting each other regardless of gender. It is a virtuous circle of success breeding more success.

Instead of holding on to the lose-lose strategy of gender inequality in which neither women nor the financial services industry benefit, let's make gender equality the win-win strategy that brings a wealth of riches to all stakeholders.

Note

1 Simone de Beauvoir (1949).

GLOSSARY OF TERMS

A

Alpha: adjective describing someone who is strong or powerful, and who likes to be in charge of others

Attribution theory: the understanding that over time, the repetitive attribution of symbolic values to each gender has become normative, influencing our perception

B

Biased investment recommendations and evaluations: internalised sexism's effect and influence on recommendations to a client

Behavioural finance: the study of the influence of psychology on the behaviour of financial professionals[1]

C

Conscious bias: the unjust influences of sex on our behaviour towards someone, when we are aware or conscious of this influence

Cultural programming: the process by which citizens come under the control of culture and what it dictates and advises

Collateralised sub-prime debts: are debts incurred when money is lent to people who are unlikely to be able to repay it, based on the promise of repayment of credit card debt, loan, mortgage, etc.

D

Digitisation: to put information into numerical form so it can be understood by a computer

Disposition effect: relates to the tendency of investors to sell assets that have increased in value, while keeping assets that have decreased in value[2]

Domestic securities: securities and assets held within the country in discussion

E

Economic theory: the ideas and principles that aim to describe how economies work

Efficient frontier: the set of optimal portfolios that offer the highest expected return for a defined level of risk or the lowest risk for a given level of expected return[3]

External orientation: placing external factors such as the needs of others as the primary motivation for investment and financial decisions

F

Financial ecosystem: the group of money management and fiscal specialist businesses that interact with and affect one another

G

Gender spectrum: the understanding that the concepts of 'male' or 'female' do not exist in a binary form and instead work on a sliding scale with these set genders and their host of associations on either end

Gender based bias/gender bias: unfair difference in the way women and men or people of other gender are treated

Gender based expectations: when gender affects your belief of what should or will occur

Group identities: an individual's perception of themselves within and relating to a community they exist within

Good enough: sense of satisfaction with expectations of oneself or others, adequate parenting or a good enough relationship

GDP: Gross domestic product: the total value of goods and services produced by a country in a year

I

Impostor syndrome: the feeling that your achievements are not real or that you do not deserve praise or success

Inflation: a general, continuous increase in prices

Interpersonal expectations: expectations of behaviour in relationships with one another

Intersectionality: the way in which different types of discrimination are linked to and affect each other

Indices: plural of index

Investment portfolio: a collection of different types of investments owned by a particular person or company

M

Market capitalisation: the total value of a company's shares on a stock market
Monoculture: a culture that is the same despite geographical location
Multidimensional: having many different features, levels or layers

N

Negative bias: our tendency to unfairly view people or a situation

O

Omega: adjective describing someone who chooses not to occupy a powerful role in a professional or social situation[4]
Operational level: relating to function
Organisational bias: when our accepted culture has undue influence on decisions
Optimised portfolio: portfolio that combines assets to produce the highest possible return at a given level of risk

P

Perceptual mismatch: a dissonance between people in their perceptions and reports of a situation
Ponzi scheme: a way of deceiving investors by using the money they give to pay interest to existing customers rather than investing it
Portfolio diversification: the risk management strategy of using a variety of assets and investments to reduce the overall risk
Psychological container: a metaphorical space in which to contain emotions and thoughts

R

Remuneration: money paid in exchange for a service
Risk and return profile: the acceptable level of risk and expected rewards that and individual is willing to accept
Rational agency theory: the understanding that as humans we have clear preferences and dislikes, out of which we will most commonly act with predictability when studied
Reverse messaging: the tweaking of the angle with which an idea is pitched to alter the way it is approached by consumers. Also showcasing diversity where it is not expected to be seen

S

Self-perceptive evaluations and judgements: our opinions and assessments of ourself

Silos: the opposite of collaboration: teams in silos do not communicate with other teams in silos

Social actors: an individual undertaking social action

Social cognitive judgements and evaluations: the way in which we acquire behaviour

Social psychology: the branch of psychology that deals with social interactions[5]

Socialisation: the process of training people to think in a way that others in the group view as suitable

Stereotype expectations: the assumption that an individual will behave in a way aligned with a set idea of a category or group, e.g., gender, race, profession that they belong to

Systemically important banks: 30 institutions where failure or large-scale loss might trigger a financial crisis[6]

Systematic malpractice: ingrained, continuous failure to act correctly or legally in the professional world, often causing injury and loss

T

Tax entities: anybody required to file tax returns

U

Unconscious bias: the unjust influences on our behaviour towards someone, when we are unaware of this influence and believe it not to be present

Unconscious gender based expectations: are those we hold when we are unaware of the expectations we maintain of people due to their gender

W

Within-gender variation: referring to the variety of different behaviours and traits between members of the same gender

Notes

1 Corporate Finance Institute (2021).
2 Weber (1995).
3 Ganti (2021).
4 Macmillan Dictionary.
5 Oxford Languages.
6 Wiki definitions.

REFERENCES

Aamidor, J., 2018. *The Latest Research Is Clear: Clean, Efficient Buildings Make People More Productive*. [Online]. Available at: https://www.greentechmedia.com/articles/read/clean-efficient-buildings-boost-worker-productivity [Accessed 27 November 2020].

Abouzahr, K., Krentz, M., Harthorne, J. & Brooks Taplett, F., 2018. *Why Women-Owned Startups Are a Better Bet*. [Online]. Available at: https://www.bcg.com/publications/2018/why-women-owned-startups-are-better-bet [Accessed 27 January 2021].

Aggarwal, R. & Boyson, N. M., 2016. The performance of female hedge fund managers. *Review of Financial Economics*, 29(1), pp. 23–36.

Agnew, J. R., Anderson, L. R., Gerlach, J. R. & Szykman, L. R., 2008. Who chooses annuities? An experimental investigation of the role of gender, framing, and defaults. *American Economic Review*, 98(2), pp. 418–22.

Allmendinger, J., cited by DW. 2021. *Parents take stock after a year of juggling responsibilities during lockdown*. [Online]. Available at: https://www.dw.com/en/parents-take-stock-after-a-year-of-juggling-responsibilities-during-lockdown/a-57109338 [Accessed 19 April 2021].

Arnold, M. & Dombey, D., 2021. *Women central bankers want action on 'hidden barriers' to equality*. The Financial Times. [Online]. Available at: https://www.ft.com/content/0d1d2d4d-8bb8-42ce-b263-9863a1f377ed?segmentId=bf7fa2fd-67ee-cdfa-8261-b2a3edbdf916 [Accessed 29 May 2021].

Avanza, 2020. *Konsten att maxa föräldraledigheten*. [Online]. Available at: https://www.avanza.se/placera/redaktionellt/2020/06/17/konsten-att-maxa-foraldraledigheten.html [Accessed 27 April 2021].

Baeckström, Y., 2020a. 'Time for the financial industry to jettison the jargon'. Professional Wealth Management. [Online] Available at:https://www.pwmnet.com/Wealth-Management/Business-Models/Private-View-Blog-Time-for-the-financial-industry-to-jettison-the-jargon?xnpe_tifc=4FHl4DxdxDbZbDBuxIx8h9psafeWaeiWhFW8ayhLtuPLhf4gVjQZadJ1Rd43tue.t9UgrFsshu4.OFsux.oZbdbZxI_T&utm_source=exponea&utm_campaign=PWM%20newsletter%2023.09.21&utm_medium=email [Accessed 23 September 2021].

Baeckström, Y., 2020b. *Investing to secure your financial future – 4 November 2019*. [Online]. Available at: https://www.kcl.ac.uk/events/investing-to-secure-your-financial-future [Accessed 30 August 2020].

Baeckström, Y., 2021. Gender based attitudes: Financial Advisor Responsiveness to Training Intervention. *(Working Paper)*.

Baeckström, Y., Silvester, J. & Pownall, R. A. J., 2018. Millionaire investors: Financial advisors, attribution theory and gender differences. *The European Journal of Finance*, 24(15), pp. 1333–49.

Baeckström, Y., Marsh, I. & Silvester, J., 2021a. Variations in investment advice provision: A study of financial advisors of millionaire investors. *Journal of Economic Behavior & Organization*, 188, pp. 716–35. https://doi.org/10.1016/j.jebo.2021.05.008.

Baeckström, Y., Marsh, I. & Silvester, J., 2021b. Financial advice and gender: Wealthy individual investors in the UK. *Journal of Corporate Finance*. https://doi.org/10.1016/j.jcorpfin.2021.101882.

Balachandra, L., Briggs, T., Eddleston, K. & Brush, C., 2019. Don't pitch like a girl!: How gender stereotypes influence investor decisions. *Entrepreneurship Theory and Practice*, 43(1), pp. 116–37. doi:10.1177/1042258717728028.

Bannier, C. & Neubert, M., 2016. Gender differences in financial risk taking: The role of financial literacy and risk tolerance. *Economics Letters*, 145(C), pp. 130–5.

Barber, B. M. & Odean, T., 1999. The courage of misguided convictions. *Financial Analysts Journal*, 55(6), pp. 41–55.

Barber, B. M. & Odean, T., 2000. Trading is hazardous to your wealth: The common stock investment performance of individual investors. *The Journal of Finance*, 55, pp. 773–806.

Barber, B. & Odean, T., 2001. Boys will be boys: Gender, overconfidence, and common stock investment. *The Quarterly Journal of Economics*, 116(1), pp. 261–92.

Benartzi, S. & Thaler, R. H., 2001. Naive diversification strategies in defined contribution saving plans. *American Economic Review*, 91(1), pp. 79–98.

Bikhchandani, S. & Sharma, S., 2001. Herd behavior in financial markets: A review. *IMF Working Paper*, 47(3), pp. 279–310.

Bilias, Y., Georgarakos, D. & Haliassos, M., 2010. Portfolio inertia and stock market fluctuations. *Journal of Money, Credit and Banking*, 42(4), pp. 715–42.

Biography, 2014a. *Ada Lovelace*. [Online]. Available at: https://www.biography.com/scholar/ada-lovelace [Accessed 07 January 2021].

Biography, 2014b. *Lewis Howard Latimer*. [Online]. Available at: https://www.biography.com/inventor/lewis-howard-latimer [Accessed 30 November 2020].

Bliss, R. T., & Potter, M. E., 2002. Mutual fund managers: Does gender matter? *The Journal of Business and Economic Studies*, 8(1), 1.

Blumberg, Y., 2018. *Companies with more female executives make more money – Here's why*. [Online]. Available at: https://www.cnbc.com/2018/03/02/why-companies-with-female-managers-make-more-money.html [Accessed 11 December 2020].

Bodenhausen, G., Macrae, C. & Sherman, J., 2016. On the dialectics of discrimination: Dual processes in social stereotyping. *Theories and Counter Models*. New York: T. G. Press.

Boston Consulting Group, 2018. *How Diverse Leadership Teams Boost Innovation*. [Online]. Available at: https://www.bcg.com/publications/2018/how-diverse-leadership-teams-boost-innovation [Accessed 28 November 2020].

Brake, 2020. [Online]. Available at: https://www.brake.org.uk/facts-resources/1593-driver-gender [Accessed 17 April 2021].

Bravata, D. M., Madhusudhan, D. K., Boroff, M. & Cokley, K. O., 2020. *Commentary: Prevalence, Predictors, and Treatment of Imposter Syndrome: A Systematic Review*. [Online]. Available at: https://www.mentalhealthjournal.org/articles/commentary-prevalence-predictors-and-treatment-of-imposter-syndrome-a-systematic-review.html [Accessed 24 October 2020].

Bremer, F., 2021. *Viktiga Årtal*. [Online]. Available at: https://www.fredrikabremer.se/om-fbf/historia/viktiga-artal/ [Accessed 22 April 2021].

Brennan, B., 2015. *Top 10 Things Everyone Should Know About Women Consumers*. [Online]. Available at: https://www.forbes.com/sites/bridgetbrennan/2015/01/21/top-10-things-everyone-should-know-about-women-consumers/?sh=782a606d6a8b [Accessed 04 August 2020].

Britannica, 2021a. *Alexander Graham Bell*. [Online]. Available at: https://www.britannica.com/biography/Alexander-Graham-Bell [Accessed 11 April 2021].

Britannica, 2021b. *Martin Cooper*. [Online]. Available at: https://www.britannica.com/biography/Martin-Cooper [Accessed 30 April 2021].

Britannica, 2021c. *Thomas Edison*. [Online]. Available at: https://www.britannica.com/biography/Thomas-Edison [Accessed 18 April 2021].

Britannica, 2021d. *Charles Babbage*. [Online]. Available at: https://www.britannica.com/biography/Charles-Babbage [Accessed 20 April 2021].

Britannica, 2021e. *William Le Baron Jenney*. [Online]. Available at: https://www.britannica.com/biography/William-Le-Baron-Jenney [Accessed 22 April 2021].

Britannica, 2021f. *Bernie Madoff*. [Online]. Available at: https://www.britannica.com/biography/Bernie-Madoff [Accessed 23 April 2021].

Brown Calder, V., 2018. *Parental Leave: Is There a Case for Government Action?*. [Online]. Available at: https://www.cato.org/policy-analysis/parental-leave-there-case-government-action [Accessed 14 August 2020].

Burke, J. & Hung, A. A., 2015. Trust and Financial Advice. *RAND Working Paper*.

Bussey, K. & Bandura, A., 1999. Social cognitive theory of gender development and differentiation. *Psychological Review*, 106(4), pp. 676–713.

Cahill, L., 2006. Why sex matters for neuroscience. *Nature Reviews Neuroscience*, 7, pp. 477–84.

Caldwell, C., Hayes, L. A., Bernal, P. & Karri, R., 2008. Ethical stewardship – Implications for leadership and trust. *Journal of Business Ethics*, 78, pp. 153–64.

Cambridge Dictionary, 2020. *Financial Services*. [Online]. Available at: https://dictionary.cambridge.org/dictionary/english/financial-services [Accessed 14 December 2020].

Cambridge Dictionary, 2021. *Overconfidence*. [Online]. Available at: https://dictionary.cambridge.org/dictionary/english/overconfidence [Accessed 10 February 2021].

Campbell, D. T., 1967. Stereotypes and the perception of group differences. *American Psychologist*, 22(10), pp. 817–29.

Campbell, J. Y. & Viceira, L. M., 2003. *Strategic Asset Allocation: Portfolio Choice for Long-Term Investors*. New York, Oxford: Oxford University Press.

Catalyst, 2017. *10 Big Issues Women Face at Work and What Leaders Can Do to Help (Blog Post)*. [Online]. Available at: https://www.catalyst.org/2017/01/19/10-big-issues-women-face-at-work-and-what-leaders-can-do-to-help/ [Accessed 2 March 2021].

Catalyst, 2020a. *Women in Financial Services (Quick Take)*. [Online]. Available at: https://www.catalyst.org/research/women-in-financial-services/ [Accessed 11 August 2020].

Catalyst, 2020b. *Women in Healthcare (Quick Take)*. [Online]. Available at: https://www.catalyst.org/research/women-in-healthcare/ [Accessed 14 December 2020].

Catalyst, 2020c. *Women in the Workforce: UK (Quick Take)*. [Online]. Available at: https://www.catalyst.org/research/women-in-the-workforce-uk/ [Accessed 25 May 2020].

Charness, G. & Gneezy, U., 2012. Strong evidence for gender differences in risk taking. *Journal of Economic Behavior & Organization*, 83(1), pp. 50–8.

Charness, G., Gneezy, U. & Imas, A., 2013. Experimental methods: Eliciting risk preferences, *Journal of Economic Behavior & Organization*, 87, pp. 43–51. https://doi.org/10.1016/j.jebo.2012.12.023.

Chef, 2020. *83 procent av Sveriges vd:ar män – Bara 17 procent kvinnor.* [Online]. Available at: https://chef.se/83-procent-av-sveriges-vdar-man-bara-17-procent-kvinnor/ [Accessed 28 August 2020].

Citigroup, 2020. *Jane Fraser – Chief Executive Officer.* [Online]. Available at: https://www.citigroup.com/citi/about/leaders/jane-fraser-bio.html [Accessed 03 December 2020].

Citizens Advice, 2021. *How much statutory maternity pay you'll get.* [Online]. Available at: https://www.citizensadvice.org.uk/work/rights-at-work/parental-rights/maternity-pay-how-much-you-can-get/ [Accessed 11 April 2021].

City of London, 2020. *UK financial services sector maintains record tax contribution.* [Online]. Available at: https://news.cityoflondon.gov.uk/uk-financial-services-sector-maintains-record-tax-contribution/ [Accessed 14 December 2020].

Colman, W., 1993. Marriage as a Psychological Container. In: *Psychotherapy with Couples.* London: Routledge, Taylor & Francis Group, p. 27.

Connelly, R. & Kimmel, J., 2003. The effect of child care costs on the employment and welfare recipiency of single mothers. *Southern Economic Journal,* 69(3), pp. 498–519.

Cooper, W., Kingyens, A. T. & Paradi, J., 2014. Two-stage financial risk tolerance assessment using data envelopment analysis. *European Journal of Operational Research,* 233(1), pp. 273–80.

Core Cashless, 2021. *The Top 3 Cashless Countries.* [Online]. Available at: https://corecashless.com/the-worlds-top-3-cashless-countries/ [Accessed 11 January 2021].

Corporate Finance Institute, 2021. *Behavioral Finance – Overview, Examples and Guide.* [Online]. Available at: https://corporatefinanceinstitute.com/resources/knowledge/trading-investing/behavioral-finance/ [Accessed 23 June 2021].

Courtenay, P., Taffler, R. & Baeckström, Y., 2021. Financial Advice or Emotional Containment? Exploring the Real Role of the Financial. *Working Paper.*

Croson, R. & Gneezy, U., 2009. Gender differences in preferences. *Journal of Economic Literature,* 47(2), pp. 1–27.

Culture Plus Consulting, 2021. *How to Develop Psychological Safety and a Speak-Up Culture.* [Online]. Available at: https://cultureplusconsulting.com/2018/03/10/how-to-develop-psychological-safety/ [Accessed 11 April 2021].

Data USA, 2021. *Covid-19 in Numbers: Finance and Insurance.* [Online]. Available at: https://datausa.io/profile/naics/finance-insurance [Accessed 17 February 2021].

Davis, K. M., 2019. *20 Facts and figures to know when marketing to women.* Forbes. [Online]. Available at: https://www.forbes.com/sites/forbescontentmarketing/2019/05/13/20-facts-and-figures-to-know-when-marketing-to-women/?sh=3861a3a71297 [Accessed 13 March 2021].

de Andrés, P., Gimeno, R. & de Cabo, R. M., 2020. The gender gap in bank credit access. *Journal of Corporate Finance,* in press.

de Beauvoir, S., 1949. [Online]. Available at: https://www.goodreads.com/author/quotes/5548.Simone_de_Beauvoir [Accessed 17 February 2021].

Del Castillo, C., 2020. *Diversity in the workplace: The case for building a diverse team.* [Online]. Available at: https://resources.workable.com/stories-and-insights/diverse-team [Accessed 13 January 2021].

Deloitte, 2019. *Within reach? Achieving gender equity in financial services leadership.* [Online]. Available at: https://www2.deloitte.com/us/en/insights/industry/financial-services/women-in-financial-services-leadership-roles.html [Accessed 23 November 2020].

Diamond, D. W. & Rajan, R. G., 2009. The credit crisis: Conjectures about causes and remedies. *American Economic Review,* 99(2), pp. 606–10.

DNB Asset Management, 2019. *Press release: Kjerstin Braathen taking over as CEO of DNB 1 September 2019.* [Online]. Available at: https://dnbam.com/en/news/press-release-kjerstin-braathen-taking-over-as-ceo-of-dnb-1-september-2019 [Accessed 22 December 2020].

Dohmen, T. et al., 2011. Individual risk attitudes: Measurement, determinants, and behavioral consequences. *Journal of the European Economic Association*, 9(3), pp. 522–50.

Duong, C., Pescetto, G. & Santamaria, D., 2014. How value–glamour investors use financial information: UK evidence of investors' confirmation bias. *The European Journal of Finance*, 20(6), pp. 524–49.

DW, 2021. *Parents take stock after a year of juggling responsibilities during lockdown.* [Online]. Available at: https://www.dw.com/en/parents-take-stock-after-a-year-of-juggling-responsibilities-during-lockdown/a-57109338 [Accessed 19 April 2021].

Dwyer, P. D., Gilkeson, J. H. & List, J. A., 2002. Gender differences in revealed risk taking: Evidence from mutual fund investors. *Economics Letters*, 76(2), pp. 151–8.

Eckel, C. & Füllbrunn, S., 2015. Thar SHE blows? Gender, competition, and bubbles in experimental asset markets. *American Economic Review*, 105(2), pp. 906–20.

Eckel, C. & Grossman, P., 2008. Forecasting risk attitudes: An experimental study using actual and forecast gamble choices. *Journal of Economic Behavior and Organization*, 68(1), pp. 1–17.

Economic Equality Impact Group, 2021. *King's College London. King's Business School.* [Online]. Available at: https://www.kcl.ac.uk/research/economic-equality-impact-group [Accessed 17 May 2021].

Edmondson, A. C., 2020. *The Role of Psychological Safety in Diversity and Inclusion.* [Online]. Available at: https://www.psychologytoday.com/us/blog/the-fearless-organization/202006/the-role-psychological-safety-in-diversity-and-inclusion [Accessed 20 February 2021].

Ekonomifakta, 2021a. *Kvinnor på arbetsmarknaden – internationellt.* [Online]. Available at: https://www.ekonomifakta.se/Fakta/Arbetsmarknad/Jamstalldhet/Kvinnor-pa-arbetsmarknaden-internationellt/ [Accessed 11 May 2021].

Ekonomifakta, 2021b. *Kvinnor i chefsposition.* [Online]. Available at: https://www.ekonomifakta.se/fakta/arbetsmarknad/jamstalldhet/kvinnor-i-chefsposition/ [Accessed 16 May 2021].

Ekonomifakta, 2021c. *Kvinnor i styrelser – internationellt.* [Online]. Available at: https://www.ekonomifakta.se/fakta/arbetsmarknad/jamstalldhet/kvinnor-i-styrelser/?-graph=/20268/1,2,3/all/ [Accessed 29 May 2021].

Eltringham, M., 2018. *How Thomas Jefferson came to invent the swivel chair and laptop.* [Online]. Available at: https://workplaceinsight.net/thomas-jefferson-came-invent-swivel-chair-laptop/ [Accessed 30 November 2020].

European Commission, 2020. *Gender Equality Strategy.* [Online]. Available at: https://ec.europa.eu/info/policies/justice-and-fundamental-rights/gender-equality/gender-equality-strategy_en [Accessed 17 May 2021].

European Commission, 2021. *International Women's Day 2021: COVID-19 pandemic is a major challenge for gender equality.* [Online]. Available at: https://ec.europa.eu/commission/presscorner/detail/en/ip_21_1011 [Accessed 12 June 2021].

Eurostat, 2019a. *Output of economic activities in the EU Member States.* [Online]. Available at: https://ec.europa.eu/eurostat/web/products-eurostat-news/-/DDN-20191028-2 [Accessed 11 December 2020].

Eurostat, 2019b. *Life expectancy at birth in the EU: Men vs. women.* [Online]. Available at: https://ec.europa.eu/eurostat/web/products-eurostat-news/-/DDN-20190725-1 [Accessed 11 August 2020].

Eurostat, 2020. *How do women and men use their time – Statistics.* [Online]. Available at: https://ec.europa.eu/eurostat/statistics-explained/index.php?title=How_do_women_and_men_use_their_time_-_statistics&oldid=463738 [Accessed 01 March 2021].

EY, 2020. *COVID-19 pandemic: How banks can increase resilience against financial crime.* [Online]. Available at: https://www.ey.com/en_gl/managed-services/covid-19-pandemic-how-banks-can-increase-resilience-against-financial-crime [Accessed 03 December 2020].

Fackförbund, 2021. *Hur länge är man föräldraledig?* [Online]. Available at: https://www.xn-fackfrbund-icb.com/vanliga-fragor/hur-lange-ar-man-foraldraledig [Accessed 3 May 2021]

Feng, L. & Seasholes, M. S., 2005. Do investor sophistication and trading experience eliminate behavioral biases in financial markets? *Review of Finance,* 9(3), pp. 305–51.

Financial Conduct Authority, 2020. *Financial Conduct Authority Handbood.* [Online]. Available at: https://www.handbook.fca.org.uk/handbook/COBS/9A/2.html [Accessed 03 January 2021].

Financial Crisis Inquiry Commission. 2011. The Financial Crisis Inquiry Report. [Online]. Available at: https://www.govinfo.gov/content/pkg/GPO-FCIC/pdf/GPO-FCIC.pdf [Accessed 11 December 2020].

Financial Stability Board (FSB), 2020. *2020 list of global systemically important banks (G-SIBs).* [Online]. Available at: https://www.fsb.org/wp-content/uploads/P111120.pdf [Accessed 04 January 2021].

Fine, C., Jordan-Young, R., Kaiser, A. & Rippon, G., 2013. Plasticity, plasticity, plasticity … and the rigid problem of sex. *Trends in Cognitive Sciences,* 17(11), pp. 550–1.

Fiske, S. T., 1993. Controlling other people: The impact of power on stereotyping. *American Psychologist,* 48(6), pp. 621–8.

Fitch Ratings, 2021. *Chinese Banks' Earnings to Stay Resilient in 2021.* [Online]. Available at: https://www.fitchratings.com/research/banks/chinese-banks-earnings-to-stay-resilient-in-2021-31-03-2021 [Accessed 19 April 2021].

Fitch, K. & Agrawal, S., 2015. *Female Bosses Are More Engaging Than Male Bosses.* [Online]. Available at: https://news.gallup.com/businessjournal/183026/female-bosses-engaging-male-bosses.aspx [Accessed 09 December 2020].

Försäkringskassan, 2021a. *Det som är bra delar man lika på.* [Online]. Available at: https://www.forsakringskassan.se/privatpers/foralder/dela-lika#:~:text=1974%20tog%20mammor%20ut%2099,och%20papporna%20cirka%2030%20procent [Accessed 03 April 2021].

Försäkringskassan, 2021b. *Föräldraledig medarbetare.* [Online]. Available at: https://www.forsakringskassan.se/arbetsgivare/foraldraledighet/foraldraledig-medarbetare [Accessed 26 April 2021].

Försäkringskassan, 2021c. *Föräldrapenning.* [Online]. Available at: https://www.forsakringskassan.se/privatpers/foralder/nar_barnet_ar_fott/foraldrapenning [Accessed 18 April 2021].

Fox & Partners, 2021. *Average pay for female FTSE-350 financial services directors just £247k vs £722k for men.* [Online]. Available at: https://www.foxlawyers.com/wp-content/uploads/2021/03/Press-Release-re.-gender-pay-gap-01.03.21.pdf [Accessed 05 April 2021].

Frable, D. E., Blackstone, T. & Scherbaum, C., 1990. Marginal and mindful: Deviants in social interactions. *Journal of Personality and Social Psychology,* 59(1), pp. 140–9.

Fraser, W., 2020. *These Are The World's 10 Highest Paying Industries.* [Online]. Available at: https://www.bosshunting.com.au/hustle/highest-paying-industries/ [Accessed 21 November 2020].

Frost & Sullivan, 2020. *Global Female Income to Reach $24 Trillion in 2020.* [Online]. Available at: https://www.prnewswire.co.uk/news-releases/global-female-income-to-reach-24-trillion-in-2020-says-frost-amp-sullivan-846488109.html [Accessed 12 May 2021].

Gallup, 2014. *The Business Benefits of Gender Diversity.* [Online]. Available at: https://www.gallup.com/workplace/236543/business-benefits-gender-diversity.aspx [Accessed 30 December 2020].

Gallup, 2018. *3 Requirements for a Diverse and Inclusive Culture.* [Online]. Available at: https://www.gallup.com/workplace/242138/requirements-diverse-inclusive-culture.aspx [Accessed 05 January 2021].

Gennaioli, N., Schleifer, A. & Vishny, R., 2015. Money doctors. *The Journal of Finance,* 70(1), pp. 91–114.

Germany Trade & Invest (GTAI), 2021. *Financial Services.* [Online]. Available at: https://www.gtai.de/gtai-en/invest/industries/financial-sector/financial-services [Accessed 23 February 2021].

Gerrans, P. & Hershey, D. A., 2017. Financial adviser anxiety, financial literacy, and financial advice seeking. *Journal of Consumer Affairs,* 51(1), pp. 54–90.

Gietl, D. & Kassner, B., 2020. Managerial overconfidence and bank bailouts. *Journal of Economic Behavior and Organization,* 179(C), pp. 202–22.

Globewomen, 2019. *2019 CWDI report on women board directors of largest banks and financial services companies globally.* [Online]. Available at: https://globewomen.org/CWDINet/index.php/2019-cwdi-report-on-women-board-directors-of-largest-banks-and-financial-services-companies-globally/ [Accessed 13 October 2020].

Gogoi, P., 2020. *Stuck-At-Home Moms: The Pandemic's Devastating Toll On Women.* [Online]. Available at: https://www.npr.org/2020/10/28/928253674/stuck-at-home-moms-the-pandemics-devastating-toll-on-women?t=1616070467956 [Accessed 23 May 2021].

Goodley, S., 2020. *Women hold a third of board roles in UK's top public companies.* [Online]. Available at: https://www.theguardian.com/business/2020/feb/08/women-hold-a-third-of-board-roles-in-uks-top-public-companies [Accessed 11 May 2021].

Stephen Jay Gould, 2021. [Online]. Available at: https://www.goodreads.com/quotes/99345-i-am-somehow-less-interested-in-the-weight-and-convolutions [Accessed 11 February 2021].

Göteborgs Stad, 2021. *Om avgifter för förskola och familjedaghem.* [Online]. Available at: https://goteborg.se/wps/portal/start/forskola-och-utbildning/forskola-o-familjedaghem/avgifter-for-forskola/avgifter [Accessed 14 March 2021].

Gov.UK, 2012. *New timetable clarifies automatic enrolment starting dates.* [Online]. Available at: https://www.gov.uk/government/news/new-timetable-clarifies-automatic-enrolment-starting-dates [Accessed 30 September 2020].

Gov.UK, 2021a. *Shared Parental Leave and Pay.* [Online]. Available at: https://www.gov.uk/shared-parental-leave-and-pay [Accessed 01 April 2021].

Gov.UK, 2021b. *Get financial help with statutory pay.* [Online]. Available at: https://www.gov.uk/recover-statutory-payments [Accessed 22 March 2021].

Gov.UK, 2021c. *30 hours free childcare.* [Online]. Available at: https://www.gov.uk/30-hours-free-childcare [Accessed 29 April 2021].

Grounds, J. N. & Haffert, K., 2020. *Do women lead differently during a crisis?* [Online]. Available at: https://www.nbcnews.com/know-your-value/feature/do-women-lead-differently-during-crisis-ncna1200506 [Accessed 22 February 2021].

Groysberg, B. & Abrahams, R., 2014. Manage your work, manage your life. *Harvard Business Review,* 92, pp. 58–66.

Gustafson, P. E., 1998. Gender differences in risk perception: Theoretical and methodological perspectives. *Risk Analysis,* 18(6), pp. 805–11.

Hackethal, A., Haliassos, M. & Jappelli, T., 2012. Financial advisors: A case of babysitters? *Journal of Banking & Finance,* 36(2), pp. 509–24.

Hake, L. & O'Connor, C., 2008. Genetic mechanisms of sex determination. *Nature Education,* 1(1):25.

Handelsbanken, 2019. *Announcement by the Board of Handelsbanken Carina Åkerström appointed new President and Group Chief Executive.* [Online]. Available at: https://news.cision.com/handelsbanken/r/announcement-by-the-board-of-handelsbanken-carina-akerstrom-appointed-new-president-and-group-chief-,c2743341 [Accessed 20 November 2020].

Harvard Kennedy School, 2021. *Venture Capital and Entrepreneurship.* [Online]. Available at: https://wappp.hks.harvard.edu/venture-capital-and-entrepreneurship [Accessed 20 April 2021].

Herman, L., 2021. *The Cold, Hard Proof That More Women Means Better Business.* [Online]. Available at: https://www.themuse.com/advice/the-cold-hard-proof-that-more-women-means-better-business [Accessed 22 February 2021].

Hermansson, C., 2018. Can self-assessed financial risk measures explain and predict bank customers' objective financial risk? *Journal of Economic Behavior & Organization,* 148, pp. 226–40.

Herring, C., 2009. Does diversity pay?: Race, gender, and the business case for diversity. *American Sociological Review,* 74(2), pp. 208–24.

Hill, J. A., Eckerd, S., Wilson, D. & Greer, B., 2009. The effect of unethical behavior on trust in a buyer–supplier relationship: The mediating role of psychological contract violation. *Journal of Operations Management,* 27(4), pp. 281–93.

Hilton, J. L. & Von Hippel, W., 1996. Stereotypes. *Annual Review of Psychology,* 47(1), pp. 237–71.

Hinchliffe, E., 2020a. *A new low for the Global 500: No women of color run businesses on this year's list.* [Online]. Available at: https://fortune.com/2020/08/10/a-new-low-for-the-global-500-no-women-of-color-run-businesses-on-this-years-list/ [Accessed 11 October 2020].

Hinchliffe, E., 2020b. *The number of female CEOs in the Fortune 500 hits an all-time record.* [Online]. Available at: https://fortune.com/2020/05/18/women-ceos-fortune-500-2020/ [Accessed 09 October 2020].

Hines, M., 2011. Gender development and the human brain. *Annual Review of Neuroscience,* 34. pp. 69–88. https://doi.org/10.1146/annurev-neuro-061010-113654.

History, 2019. *Bank Run.* [Online]. Available at: https://www.history.com/topics/great-depression/bank-run [Accessed 16 February 2021].

History Collection, 2019. *40 Basic Rights Women Did Not Have Until The 1970s.* [Online]. Available at: https://historycollection.com/40-basic-rights-women-did-not-have-until-the-1970s/30/ [Accessed 16 November 2020].

Hoechle, D., Ruenzi, S., Schaub, N. & Schmid, M., 2017. The impact of financial advice on trade performance and behavioral biases. *Review of Finance,* 21(2), pp. 871–910.

Hoffmann, A. O. I. & Post, T., 2014. Self-attribution bias in consumer financial decision-making: How investment returns affect individuals' belief in skill. *Journal of Behavioral and Experimental Economics,* 52, pp. 23–8.

Homan, A. C., Gündemir, S., Buengeler, C. & Van Kleef, G. A., 2020. Leading diversity: Towards a theory of functional leadership in diverse teams. *Journal of Applied Psychology,* 105(10), pp. 1101–28.

Hong, H., Kubik, J. D. & Stein, J. C., 2004. Social interaction and stock-market participation. *The Journal of Finance,* 59(1), pp. 137–63.

Howe, S., 2021. *Famous Fraudsters – The Originator Of The Modern Ponzi Scheme.* [Online]. Available at: https://www.fraugster.com/resources/post/famous-fraudsters-sarah-howe [Accessed 12 May 2021].

Hurtado, A., 1997. *The Color of Privilege: Three Blasphemies on Race and Feminism.* Ann Arbor, MI: University of Michigan Press.

Inderst, R. & Ottaviani, M., 2012. How (not) to pay for advice: A framework for consumer financial protection. *Journal of Financial Economics,* 105(2), pp. 393–411.

Inman, P., 2018. *Treasury chooses only man on shortlist of five for Bank of England job.* [Online]. Available at: https://www.theguardian.com/business/2018/may/31/bank-of-england-picks-the-only-man-on-a-shortlist-of-candidates [Accessed 23 August 2020].

International Labour Organization (ILO), 2020. *World Employment and Social Outlook: Which sector will create the most jobs?.* [Online]. Available at: https://www.ilo.org/global/about-the-ilo/multimedia/maps-and-charts/WCMS_337082/lang-en/index.htm [Accessed 23 January 2021].

International Monetary Fund (IMF), 2020. *Gender-balanced Leadership: Guarding Financial Stability in Crisis Times.* [Online]. Available at: https://www.imf.org/en/News/Articles/2020/06/10/sp061020-gender-balanced-leadership-guarding-financial-stability-in-crisis-times [Accessed 25 April 2021].

Investopedia, 2019. *How London Became the World's Financial Hub.* [Online]. Available at: https://www.investopedia.com/how-london-became-the-world-s-financial-hub-4589324 [Accessed 03 September 2020].

Investopedia, 2020a. *Financial Services: Sizing the Sector in the Global Economy.* [Online]. Available at: https://www.investopedia.com/ask/answers/030515/what-percentage-global-economy-comprised-financial-services-sector.asp [Accessed 17 March 2021].

Investopedia, 2020b. *Foreign Institutional Investor (FII).* [Online]. Available at: https://www.investopedia.com/terms/f/fii.asp [Accessed 19 February 2021].

Investopedia, 2021a. *Akhilesh Ganti.* [Online]. Available at: https://www.investopedia.com/akhilesh-ganti-4590113 [Accessed 28 May 2021].

Investopedia, 2021b. *Long-Term Capital Management (LTCM).* [Online]. Available at: https://www.investopedia.com/terms/l/longtermcapital.asp [Accessed 04 March 2021].

Investopedia, 2021c. *The LIBOR Scandal.* [Online]. Available at: https://www.investopedia.com/terms/l/libor-scandal.asp [Accessed 23 April 2021].

Jensen, M. C. & Meckling, W. H., 1976. Theory of the firm: Managerial behavior, agency costs and ownership. *Journal of Financial Economics*, 3, pp. 305–60.

Johnson, J. E. V. & Powell, P. L., 1994. Decision making, risk and gender: Are managers different? *British Journal of Management*, 5(2), pp. 123–38.

Jones, A., 2021. *What Brexit means for the UK's financial services sector.* [Online]. Available at: https://internationalbanker.com/finance/what-brexit-means-for-the-uks-financial-services-sector/ [Accessed 11 May 2021].

Jones, L. & Baeckström, Y., 2020. *The visibility of women in the UK business and finance press.* [Online]. Available at: https://www.kcl.ac.uk/giwl/assets/visibility-of-women-in-the-uk-business-and-finance-press.pdf [Accessed 17 November 2020].

Joseph, B., 1987. *Projective Identification: Clinical Aspects*, 1st edition. London: Routledge. p. 12.

Joshi, A., Liao, H. & Jackso, S. E., 2016. Cross-level effects of workplace diversity on sales performance and pay. *Academy of Management Journal*, 49(3), pp. 459–81.

JP Morgan Chase, 2021. *JP Morgan Chase (2021) Press release JP Morgan Chase reports fourth-quarter 2020....* [Online]. Available at: https://www.jpmorganchase.com/content/dam/jpmc/jpmorgan-chase-and-co/investor-relations/documents/quarterly-earnings/2020/4th-quarter/276305ed-730d-4acc-887c-1671d6c39e53.pdf [Accessed 02 June 2021].

Kahneman, D., 2003. Maps of bounded rationality: Psychology for behavioral economics. *American Economic Review*, 93(5), pp. 1449–75.

Kahneman, D., & Tversky, A. 1973. On the psychology of prediction. *Psychological Review*, 80(4), pp. 237–51.

Kahneman, D. & Tversky, A., 1979. Prospect theory: An analysis of decision under risk. *Econometrica*, 47(2), pp. 263–92.

Kantar, 2021. *The Reykjavik Index for Leadership 2020/2021*. [Online]. Available at: https://www.kantar.com/campaigns/reykjavik-index [Accessed 28 May 2021].

Kelley, H. H., 1973. The processes of causal attribution. *American Psychologist*, 28(2), pp. 107–28.

Kohli, R., 2018. *Women & Banking: India's financial inclusion suffers from a gender gap.* [Online]. Available at: https://www.financialexpress.com/opinion/women-banking-indias-financial-inclusion-suffers-from-a-gender-gap/1173467/ [Accessed 20 November 2020].

KPMG, 2020a. *COVID-19 Insights – Emerging Risks: Financial services sector is having to adapt rapidly.* [Online]. Available at: https://home.kpmg/xx/en/home/insights/2020/04/covid-19-insights-emerging-risks.html [Accessed 03 November 2020].

KPMG, 2020b. *Payments deals forge ahead despite COVID-19.* [Online]. Available at: https://home.kpmg/xx/en/blogs/home/posts/2020/07/payments-deals-soar-despite-covid-19.html [Accessed 01 September 2021].

Kramer, M. M., 2012. Financial advice and individual investor portfolio performance. *Financial Management*, 41(2), pp. 395–428.

Kramer, M. M., 2016. Financial literacy, confidence and financial advice seeking. *Journal of Economic Behavior & Organization*, 131, pp. 198–217.

Kremer, S. & Nautz, D., 2013. Causes and consequences of short-term institutional herding. *Journal of Banking & Finance*, 37(5), pp. 1676–86.

Lagarde, C., 2014. *The Economic Power of Women's Empowerment, Keynote Speech By Christine Lagarde, Managing Director, International Monetary Fund.* [Online]. Available at: https://www.imf.org/en/News/Articles/2015/09/28/04/53/sp091214 [Accessed 29 December 2020].

Lambert, P. A., 2008. The comparative political economy of parental leave and child care: Evidence from twenty OECD countries. *Social Politics: International Studies in Gender, State & Society*, 15(3), pp. 315–44.

Lighthall, N. R., Mather, M. & Gorlick, M. A., 2009. Acute stress increases sex differences in risk seeking in the balloon analogue risk task. *PLOS One*, 4(7), e6002.

Loewenstein, G. F., Weber, E. U., Hsee, C. K. & Welch, N., 2001. Risk as feelings. *Psychological Bulletin*, 127, pp. 267–86.

LogoMyWay, 2021. *Popular Bank Logos.* [Online]. Available at: https://blog.logomyway.com/popular-bank-logos/ [Accessed 13 February 2021].

Lusardi, A. & Mitchell, O. S., 2007. Baby boomer retirement security: The roles of. *Journal of Monetary Economics*, 54, pp. 205–24.

Madrian, B. C. & Shea, D. F., 2001. The power of suggestion: Inertia in 401(k) participation and savings behavior. *The Quarterly Journal of Economics*, 116(4), pp. 1149–87.

Malle, B. F., 2006. The actor-observer asymmetry in attribution: A (surprising) meta-analysis. *Psychological Bulletin*, 132(6), pp. 895–919.

Markowitz, H., 1952. Portfolio selection. *The Journal of Finance*, 7(1), pp. 77–91.

Markowitz, H., 2010. Portfolio theory: As I still see it. *Annual Review of Financial Economics*, 1, pp. 1–23.

MasterCard, 2018. *Europe leads contactless adoption as almost 1 in 2 transactions are now contactless.* [Online]. Available at: https://newsroom.mastercard.com/eu/press-releases/europe-leads-contactless-adoption-as-almost-1-in-2-transactions-are-now-contactless/ [Accessed 12 March 2021].

McCulloch, A., 2020. *UK banks increase number of female board members.* [Online]. Available at: https://www.personneltoday.com/hr/uk-banks-increase-number-of-female-board-members/ [Accessed 22 October 2020].

McKinsey & Company, 2015. *Why diversity matters.* [Online]. Available at: https://www.mckinsey.com/business-functions/organization/our-insights/why-diversity-matters [Accessed 28 August 2020].

McKinsey & Company, 2017. *Women Matter: Time to accelerate: Ten years of insights into gender diversity.* [Online]. Available at: https://www.mckinsey.com/~/media/mckinsey/featured%20insights/women%20matter/women%20matter%20ten%20years%20of%20insights%20on%20the%20importance%20of%20gender%20diversity/women-matter-time-to-accelerate-ten-years-of-insights-into-gender-diversity.pdf [Accessed 11 May 2021].

McKinsey Global Institute, 2015. *How advancing women's equality can add $12 trillion to global growth.* [Online]. Available at: https://www.mckinsey.com/featured-insights/employment-and-growth/how-advancing-womens-equality-can-add-12-trillion-to-global-growth# [Accessed 26 April 2021].

McLeod, N., 2014. Tending the Fire. In: *Masculindians: Conversations about Indigenous Manhood.* 1st edition, McKegney, S., ed., M. S. U. Press. p. 256.

Merton, Robert C., 1969. Lifetime Portfolio Selection under Uncertainty: The Continuous-Time Case. *The Review of Economics and Statistics*, 51(3), pp. 247.

Moise, I., 2021. *JPMorgan earnings surge on strengthening US economy.* The Financial Times. [Online]. Available at: https://www.ft.com/content/0595526e-48fa-48ff-a594-d219f15b54a4 [Accessed 15 May 2021].

Moise, I. & Morris, S., 2021. *US and Europe split on bringing bankers back to the office.* The Financial Times. [Online]. Available at: https://www.ft.com/content/547a4dc2-e11b-4e8f-b526-cbf135ba7b4d [Accessed 13 April 2021].

Moncrief, W. C., Babakus, E., Cravens, D. W. & Johnston, M. W., 2000. Examining gender differences in field sales organizations. *Journal of Business Research*, 49(3), pp. 245–57.

Money and Pensions Service. 2019, Conference presentation, London July 2019.

Morris, S. & Megaw, N., 2018. *RBS drops off list of world's most important banks.* The Financial Times. [Online]. Available at: https://www.ft.com/content/3a23cd6c-e999-11e8-a34c-663b3f553b35 [Accessed 28 November 2020].

Mullainathan, S., Noeth, M. & Schoar, A., 2012. The market for financial advice: An audit study. *National Bureau of Economic Research.*

National Women's History Museum, 2020. *Muriel Siebert.* [Online]. Available at: https://www.womenshistory.org/education-resources/biographies/muriel-siebert [Accessed 27 January 2021].

Neelakantan, U., 2010. Estimation and impact of gender differences in risk tolerance. *Economic Inquiry*, 48(1), pp. 228–33.

Nelson, J. A., 2015. Are women really more risk-averse than men? A re-analysis of the literature using expanded methods. *Journal of Economic Surveys*, 29(3), pp. 566–85.

Niessen-Ruenzi, A. & Ruenzi, S., 2018. Sex matters: Gender bias in the mutual fund industry. *Management Science*, 65(7), pp. 2947–3448.

Nisbett, R. E. & Wilson, T. D., 1977. Telling more than we can know: Verbal reports on mental processes. *Psychological Review*, 84(3), pp. 231–59.

Noja, G. G., Thalassinos, E. I., Cristea, M. & Grecu, I. M., 2021. The interplay between board characteristics, financial performance, and risk management disclosure in the financial services sector: New empirical evidence from Europe. *Journal of Risk and Financial Management*, 14(2), 79.

Nonninger, L., 2019. *Digital financial services in Southeast Asia will triple to $38 billion in revenue by 2025.* [Online]. Available at: https://www.businessinsider.com/southeast-asia-financial-services-revenue-will-triple-by-2025-2019-11?r=US&IR=T [Accessed 11 September 2020].

Norwood, A. R., 2017. *Maggie Lena Walker.* [Online]. Available at: https://www.womenshistory.org/education-resources/biographies/maggie-lena-walker [Accessed 11 January 2021].

OECD, 2019. *Pension Markets in Focus.* [Online]. Available at: https://www.oecd.org/daf/fin/private-pensions/Pension-Markets-in-Focus-2019.pdf [Accessed 28 August 2020].

OECD, 2020. *Inflation (CPI).* [Online]. Available at: https://data.oecd.org/price/inflation-cpi.htm [Accessed 15 November 2020].

OECD, 2021. *Global pension statistics.* [Online]. Available at: https://www.oecd.org/daf/fin/private-pensions/globalpensionstatistics.htm [Accessed 16 June 2021].

Office for National Statistics, 2019. *Gender pay gap in the UK: 2019.* [Online]. Available at: https://www.ons.gov.uk/employmentandlabourmarket/peopleinwork/earningsandworkinghours/bulletins/genderpaygapintheuk/2019 [Accessed 14 December 2020].

Office for National Statistics, 2021. *Coronavirus and the impact on output in the UK economy: December 2020.* [Online]. Available at: https://www.ons.gov.uk/economy/grossdomesticproductgdp/articles/coronavirusandtheimpactonoutputintheukeconomy/december2020#:~:text=6.-,The%20UK%20economy%20during%20the%20coronavirus%20(COVID%2D19)%20pandemic,to%20the%20measurement%20of%20GDP [Accessed 09 March 2021].

Office for National Statistics, 2021a. *EARN03: Average weekly earnings by industry.* [Online]. Available at: https://www.ons.gov.uk/employmentandlabourmarket/peopleinwork/earningsandworkinghours/datasets/averageweeklyearningsbyindustryearn03 [Accessed 22 June 2021].

Oliver Wyman, 2020. *Asia Finance 2020: Framing A New Asian Financial Architecture.* [Online]. Available at: https://www.oliverwyman.com/content/dam/oliver-wyman/global/en/files/archive/2013/Asia_Finance_2020.pdf [Accessed 27 January 2021].

On Average, 2021. *Average Salary UK.* [Online]. Available at: https://www.onaverage.co.uk/money-averages/average-salary-uk [Accessed 01 May 2021].

Osakwe, A., 2018. *Meet the first woman to lead the NYSE in 226 years.* [Online]. Available at: https://abcnews.go.com/GMA/News/meet-woman-lead-nyse-226-years/story?id=55351824 [Accessed 09 September 2020].

Overseas Development Institute, 2016. *Women's work: Mothers, children and the global childcare crisis.* [Online]. Available at: https://bettercarenetwork.org/sites/default/files/Women%E2%80%99s%20work-%20Mothers%2C%20children%20and%20the%20global%20childcare%20crisis.pdf [Accessed 08 April 2021].

Oyer, P. 2008, The making of an investment banker: Stock market shocks, career choice, and lifetime income. *The Journal of Finance,* 63: 2601–28. https://doi.org/10.1111/j.1540-6261.2008.01409.x.

Partridge, M., 2019. *Great frauds in history: Adelheid Luise Spitzeder.* [Online]. Available at: https://moneyweek.com/511836/great-frauds-in-history-adelheid-luise-spitzeder [Accessed 24 May 2021].

Payscale, 2021. *The State of the Gender Pay Gap in 2021.* [Online]. Available at: https://www.payscale.com/data/gender-pay-gap [Accessed 11 May 2021].

Petter, O., 2019. *Fewer Than Third of New Fathers Take Paternity Leave, Research Suggests.* [Online]. Available at: https://www.independent.co.uk/life-style/health-and-families/paternity-leave-new-fathers-less-third-not-taking-a8992086.html [Accessed 03 November 2020].

Pikulina, E., Renneboog, L. & Tobler, P. N., 2017. Overconfidence and investment: An experimental approach. *Journal of Corporate Finance,* 43(C), pp. 175–92.

Post, S., 2020. *Improving Team Performance: How Gender Diversity Benefits the Workplace.* [Online]. Available at: https://www.securitymagazine.com/articles/91908-improving-team-performance-how-gender-diversity-benefits-the-workplace [Accessed 11 January 2021].

PwC, 2021. *Global M&A Industry Trends.* [Online]. Available at: https://www.pwc.com/gx/en/services/deals/trends.html [Accessed 11 March 2021].

Ragins, B. R. & Sundstrom, E., 1989. Gender and power in organizations: A longitudinal perspective. *Psychological Bulletin*, 105(1), pp. 51–88.

Riefler, R. & Baeckström, Y., 2020. Examining Gender Differences in Sales Performance: Institutional Financial Brokerage. Working Paper.

Ro, C., 2021. *Why do we still distrust women leaders?* [Online]. Available at: https://www.bbc.com/worklife/article/20210108-why-do-we-still-distrust-women-leaders [Accessed 11 March 2021].

Romei, V., 2021. 'I am close to quitting my career': Mothers step back at work to cope with pandemic parenting. [Online]. Available at: https://www.ft.com/content/d5d01f06-9f7c-4cdc-9fee-225e15b5750b?segmentId=bf7fa2fd-67ee-cdfa-8261-b2a3edbdf916 [Accessed 13 May 2021].

Rosen, S., 2020. *How Ruth Bader Ginsburg Paved the Way for Women to Get Credit Cards.* [Online]. Available at: https://time.com/nextadvisor/credit-cards/ruth-bader-ginsburg-credit-card-legacy/ [Accessed 12 December 2020].

Rosen, H. S. & Wu, S., 2004. Portfolio choice and health status. *Journal of Financial Economics*, 72(3), pp. 457–84.

Ross, S. A., 1973. The economic theory of agency: The principal's problem. *The American Economic Review*, 63, pp. 134–9.

Rosser, W. W. & Kasperski, J., 2001. The benefits of a trusting physician-patient relationship. *The Journal of family practice*, 50(4), pp. 329–30.

Salary Explorer, 2021. *Banking Average Salaries in United Kingdom 2021.* [Online]. Available at: http://www.salaryexplorer.com/salary-survey.php?loc=228&loctype=1&job=13&jobtype=1 [Accessed 11 June 2021].

Samuelson, P. A., 1989. A Case at Last for Age-Phased Reduction in Equity. *Proceedings of the National Academy of Sciences*, 86(22), pp. 9048–51.

Sappington, D. E., 1991. Incentives in principal-agent relationships. *Journal of Economic Perspectives*, 5(2), pp. 45–66.

Scandura, T. A. & Viator, R. E., 1994. Mentoring in public accounting firms: An analysis of mentor-protégé relationships, mentorship functions, and protégé turnover intentions. *Accounting, Organizations and Society*, 19(8), pp. 717–34.

Scheff, T. J., 2003. Male Emotions/Relationships and violence: A case study. *Human Relations*, 56(6), pp. 727–49.

Select USA, 2021. *Financial Services Spotlight: The Financial Services Industry in the United States.* [Online]. Available at: https://www.selectusa.gov/financial-services-industry-united-states [Accessed 12 May 2021].

Shah, A., 2017. *Women's hands really are colder than men's, scientists confirm.* [Online]. Available at: https://medicalxpress.com/news/2017-12-women-colder-men-scientists.html [Accessed 05 December 2020].

Shapiro, G. K. & Burchell, B., 2012. Measuring financial anxiety. *Journal of Neuroscience, Psychology, and Economics*, 5(2), pp. 92–103.

Shefrin, H. & Statman, M., 1985. The disposition to sell winners too early and ride losers too long: Theory and evidence. *The Journal of Finance*, 40(3), pp. 777–90.

Shiller, R. J., 2000. *Irrational Exuberance.* Princeton, New Jersey: Princeton University Press, pp. 149–53.

Shiller, R. J., 2003. From efficient markets theory to behavioral finance. *Journal of Economic Perspectives*, 17(1), 83–104.

Shirley, S., 2021. *Personal Website.* [Online]. Available at: https://www.steveshirley.com/ [Accessed 03 June 2021].

Silverberg, T., 2021. *The History of Women and Money in the United States in Honor of Women's History Month*. [Online]. Available at: https://www.oneadvisorypartners.com/blog/the-history-of-women-and-money-in-the-united-states-in-honor-of-womens-history-month [Accessed 13 February 2021].

Silverstein, M. J. & Sayre, K., 2009. *The Female Economy*. [Online]. Available at: https://hbr.org/2009/09/the-female-economy [Accessed 19 November 2020].

Silvester, J. & Koczwara, A., 2012. Explaining Male and Female Leadership Potential: New York and London. *Paper presented at the Society for Industrial & Organizational Psychology Annual Conference, San Diego, U.S.*

Simmons and Simmons, 2018. *Timeline released for opening up of China's financial services sector to foreign investors.* [Online]. Available at: https://www.simmons-simmons.com/en/publications/ck0a6jxc46gb10b94mnbn59tu/120418-china-financial-services-sector-timeline-4si4p4c [Accessed 29 August 2020].

Smith, E., 2021. *Deutsche Bank reports its best quarterly profit for seven years.* [Online]. Available at: https://www.cnbc.com/2021/04/28/deutsche-bank-earnings-q1-2021.html [Accessed 22 April 2021].

Song, F. & Thakor, A. V., 2019. Bank culture. *Journal of Financial Intermediation*, 39, pp. 59–79.

Statista, 2020. *Life expectancy in industrial and developing countries.* [Online]. Available at: https://www.statista.com/statistics/274507/life-expectancy-in-industrial-and-developing-countries/ [Accessed 09 September 2020].

Statista, 2021a. *Global gross domestic product (GDP) at current prices from 1985 to 2026.* [Online]. Available at: https://www.statista.com/statistics/268750/global-gross-domestic-product-gdp/ [Accessed 14 June 2021].

Statista, 2021b. *European finance and insurance services sector value added as a percentage of the total economic output in 2019, by country.* [Online]. Available at: https://www.statista.com/statistics/1120958/european-financial-sector-value-added-share-of-total-economy-by-country/ [Accessed 14 March 2021].

Statista, 2021c. *Gross domestic product at current market prices of selected European countries in 2020.* [Online]. Available at: https://www.statista.com/statistics/685925/gdp-of-european-countries/ [Accessed 11 June 2021].

Statista, 2021d. *Leading ten financial centers in Asia Pacific in 2020, by city.* [Online]. Available at: https://www.statista.com/statistics/380608/leading-financial-centers-asia-pacific/#:~:text=Leading%20ten%20financial%20centers%20APAC%202019&text=In%202019%2C%20Tokyo%20proved%20to,financial%20center%20ranking%20in%202019. [Accessed 28 May 2021].

Statista, 2021e. *Banking in Europe – Statistics & Facts.* [Online]. Available at: https://www.statista.com/topics/3426/banking-sector-in-europe/ [Accessed 10 June 2021].

Stewart, A. J. & McDermott, C., 2004. Gender in psychology. *Annual Review of Psychology*, 55, pp. 519–44.

Striking Women, 2021. *Maternity (and paternity) leave and pay.* [Online]. Available at: https://www.striking-women.org/module/workplace-issues-past-and-present/maternity-and-paternity-leave-and-pay [Accessed 02 April 2021].

Sunden, A. E. & Surette, B. J., 1998. Gender differences in the allocation of assets in retirement savings plans. *American Economic Review*, 88(2), pp. 207–11.

Sunderland, R., 2009. *The real victims of this credit crunch? Women.* [Online]. Available at: https://www.theguardian.com/lifeandstyle/2009/jan/18/women-credit-crunch-ruth-sunderland [Accessed 26 August 2020].

Sveriges Riksbank, 2020. *1. The payment market is being digitalised.* [Online]. Available at: https://www.riksbank.se/en-gb/payments-cash/payments-in-sweden/payments-in-sweden-2020/1.-the-payment-market-is-being-digitalised/cash-is-losing-ground/ [Accessed 28 December 2020].

Sweden.com, 2021. *Equal power and influence for women and men – that's what Sweden is aiming for.* [Online]. Available at: https://sweden.se/life/equality/gender-equality

Swedish Community for Sustainable Finance, 2021. *New community with focus on sustainable finance.* [Online]. Available at: https://www.gu.se/en/news/new-community-with-focus-on-sustainable-finance [Accessed 27 May 2021].

Tax and the Family, 2021. *History.* [Online]. Available at: https://www.taxandthefamily.org/history-article [Accessed 06 March 2021].

Taylor, C., 2019. *Having more female leaders may boost companies' share price performance, Credit Suisse says.* [Online]. Available at: https://www.cnbc.com/2019/10/14/female-leaders-may-boost-share-price-performance-credit-suisse-says.html [Accessed 30 November 2020].

Teare, G., 2020. *Global VC funding to female founders dropped dramatically this year.* [Online]. Available at: https://news.crunchbase.com/news/global-vc-funding-to-female-founders/ [Accessed 30 may 2021].

The Baring Archive, 2021. *A Brief History of Barings.* [Online]. Available at: https://www.baringarchive.org.uk/history/a_brief_history_of_barings/ [Accessed 31 October 2021].

The Business Research Company, 2020. *Financial Services Global Market Report 2021: COVID-19 Impact and Recovery To 2030.* [Online]. Available at: https://www.thebusinessresearchcompany.com/report/financial-services-global-market-report-2020-30-covid-19-impact-and-recovery [Accessed 24 February 2021].

The City UK, 2018. *Key facts about the UK as an international financial centre 2018.* [Online]. Available at: https://www.thecityuk.com/research/key-facts-about-the-uk-as-an-international-financial-centre-2018/ [Accessed 10 August 2020].

The Conversation, 2018. *Women's unpaid work must be included in GDP calculations: Lessons from history.* [Online]. Available at: https://theconversation.com/womens-unpaid-work-must-be-included-in-gdp-calculations-lessons-from-history-98110 [Accessed 29 September 2020].

The Economist, 2009. *Women in the workforce: The Female Power.* [Online] Available at: https://www.economist.com/briefing/2009/12/30/female-power [Accessed 15 November 2020].

The Economist, 2021. *Profits at America's banks are sky-high.* [Online]. Available at: https://www.economist.com/finance-and-economics/2021/04/17/profits-at-americas-banks-are-sky-high [Accessed 13 May 2021].

Thomas, D. & Megaw, N., 2020. *RBS tells majority of staff to work from home until 2021.* The Financial Times. [Online]. Available at: https://www.ft.com/content/45de5b8d-4c93-4288-b44a-d272e2173efe [Accessed 14 April 2021].

The Guardian, 2009. https://www.theguardian.com/lifeandstyle/2009/jan/18/women-credit-crunch-ruth-sunderland. Ruth Sunderland 18 Jan 2009. The real victims of this credit crunch? Women.

The Global Economy, 2017. *Percent people with credit cards – Country rankings.* [Online]. Available at: https://www.theglobaleconomy.com/rankings/people_with_credit_cards/ [Accessed 13 March 2021].

The Money Advice Service, 2021a. *What is Statutory Maternity Pay?* [Online]. Available at: https://www.moneyadviceservice.org.uk/en/articles/maternity-pay-and-leave [Accessed 22 March 2021].

The Money Advice Service, 2021b. *Paternity pay.* [Online]. Available at: https://www.moneyadviceservice.org.uk/en/articles/paternity-leave-and-pay [Accessed 22 March 2021].

The Money Advice Service, 2021c. *What benefits can I claim when I'm pregnant or have a baby?*. [Online]. Available at: https://www.moneyadviceservice.org.uk/en/articles/benefits-and-entitlements-to-claim-when-you-have-a-baby [Accessed 23 March 2021].

The Telegraph, 2018. *1918 vs 2018 – 13 things women couldn't do 100 years ago.* [Online]. Available at: https://www.telegraph.co.uk/women/life/1918-vs-2018-13-things-women-couldnt-do-100-years-ago/ [Accessed 25 August 2020].

The World Bank, 2014. *Expanding Women's Access to Financial Services.* [Online]. Available at: https://www.worldbank.org/en/results/2013/04/01/banking-on-women-extending-womens-access-to-financial-services [Accessed 19 August 2020].

The World Bank, 2017. *The Global Findex Database 2017.* [Online]. Available at: https://globalfindex.worldbank.org/ [Accessed 14 November 2020].

The World Bank, 2020a. *World Bank national accounts data, and OECD National Accounts data files.* [Online]. Available at: https://data.worldbank.org/indicator/NY.GDP.MKTP.CD?locations=CN-GB [Accessed 13 October 2020].

The World Bank, 2020b. *40 Economies Make 62 Legal Reforms to Advance Women's Economic Participation.* [Online]. Available at: https://www.worldbank.org/en/news/press-release/2020/01/14/40-economies-make-62-legal-reforms-to-advance-womens-economic-participation [Accessed 28 August 2021].

The World Bank, 2020c. *Financial Sector.* [Online]. Available at: https://www.worldbank.org/en/topic/financialsector/overview [Accessed 02 March 2021].

The World Bank Group, 2020. *Women, Business and the Law 2020.* [Online]. Available at: https://openknowledge.worldbank.org/bitstream/handle/10986/32639/9781464815324.pdf?sequence=10 [Accessed 30 January 2021].

The World Bank Group, 2021. *Women, Business and the Law 2021.* [Online]. Available at: https://openknowledge.worldbank.org/bitstream/handle/10986/35094/9781464816529.pdf [Accessed 12 June 2021].

The World Economic Forum, 2020d. *COVID-19 has widened the gender poverty gap, says the UN.* [Online]. Available at: https://www.weforum.org/agenda/2020/09/covid19-women-pandemic-gender-poverty-gap-united-nations [Accessed 09 October 2020].

The World Economic Forum, 2020a. *Global Gender Gap Report 2020.* [Online]. Available at: http://www3.weforum.org/docs/WEF_GGGR_2020.pdf [Accessed 01 February 2021].

The World Economic Forum, 2020b. *Hardwiring Gender Parity in the Future of Work.* [Online]. Available at: https://www.weforum.org/projects/hardwiring-gender-parity-in-the-future-of-work [Accessed 10 August 2020].

The World Economic Forum, 2020c. *Global Gender Gap Report 2020.* [Online]. https://www.weforum.org/reports/gender-gap-2020-report-100-years-pay-equality [Accessed 1 April 2021]

Their World, 2021. *More chores for British girls means less time for schoolwork.* [Online]. Available at: https://theirworld.org/news/british-girls-doing-more-chores-less-schoolwork-in-lockdown [Accessed 28 April 2021].

Tucker, J. J. III & Jones, S., 2019. Diversity continues to challenge the financial services industry: Benefits, financial performance, demographics, impediments to progress, and Best practices. *Journal of Financial Service Professionals*, 73(1), pp. 56–71.

Turban, S., Wu, D. & Zhang, L., 2019. *Research: When Gender Diversity Makes Firms More Productive.* [Online]. Available at: https://hbr.org/2019/02/research-when-gender-diversity-makes-firms-more-productive [Accessed 28 September 2020].

Tversky, A. & Kahneman, D., 1986. The framing of decisions and the evaluation of prospects. *Studies in Logic and the Foundations of Mathematics*, 114, pp. 503–20.

Udry, R. J., 2000. Biological limits of gender construction. *American Sociological Review*, 65(3), pp. 443–57.

UK Parliament, 2021a. *Financial Services: Contribution to the UK Economy.* [Online]. Available at: https://commonslibrary.parliament.uk/research-briefings/sn06193/ [Accessed 16 May 2021].

UK Parliament, 2021b. *Women and the economy.* [Online]. Available at: https://commonslibrary.parliament.uk/research-briefings/sn06838/ [Accessed 11 May 2021].

UN News, 2014. *Equality for women means progress for all, UN officials declare, marking International Day.* [Online]. Available at: https://news.un.org/en/story/2014/03/463472-equality-women-means-progress-all-un-officials-declare-marking-international [Accessed 15 December 2020].

UN News, 2021. [Online]. Available at: https://news.un.org/en/story/2021/03/1087392 [Accessed 21 April 2021].

UN Women, 2020. *Equal pay for work of equal value.* [Online]. Available at: https://www.unwomen.org/en/news/in-focus/csw61/equal-pay [Accessed 01 April 2021].

Unicef, 2021. *Redesigning the workplace to be family-friendly: What governments and businesses can do.* [Online]. Available at: https://www.unicef.org/early-childhood-development/family-friendly-policies [Accessed 29 May 2021].

USA News, 2021. *Best Countries for Raising Kids.* [Online]. Available at: https://www.usnews.com/news/best-countries/best-countries-to-raise-a-family [Accessed 27 March 2021].

Velati, A., 2021. *Morgan Stanley chief talks tough on return to the office.* [Online]. Available at: https://www.ft.com/content/ffd6033f-e8fc-4289-85b2-42bc4ddddd16 [Accessed 16 June 2021].

Walker, O., 2018. *Fund managers forced to confront endemic gender pay gap.* The Financial Times, [Online]. Available at: https://www.ft.com/content/8eebbc76-38d0-11e8-8b98-2f31af407cc8 [Accessed 27 August 2020].

Walker, M. L., 2019. *Early Women In Banking.* [Online]. Available at: https://www.nps.gov/mawa/learn/historyculture/female-bank-presidents.htm [Accessed 11 November 2020].

Walsh, J., 2012. Not worth the sacrifice? Women's aspirations and career progression in law firms. *Gender, Work & Organization,* 19(5), pp. 508–31.

Wärneryd, K.-E., 1996. Risk attitudes and risky behavior. *Journal of Economic Psychology,* 17(6), pp. 749–70.

Wealth-X, 2020. *A Decade of Wealth: A Review of the Past 10 Years in Wealth and a Look Forward to the Decade to Come.* [Online]. Available at: https://www.wealthx.com/report/decade-of-wealth/#downloadform [Accessed 11 January 2021].

Weber, M., 1995. The disposition effect in securities trading: An experimental Analysis. *Journal of Economic Behavior & Organization,* 33(2), pp. 167–84.

Weedston, L., 2016. *10 Black Women Innovators and the Awesome Things They Brought Us.* [Online]. Available at: https://www.yesmagazine.org/health-happiness/2016/03/21/10-black-women-innovators-and-the-awesome-things-they-brought-us [Accessed 13 December 2020].

Weiner, B., Frieze, I., Kukla, A. & Rosenbaum, R. M., 1971. Perceiving the causes of success and failure. *Developmental Psychology,* 11(1), p. 103.

Weisman, S., 2020. *The History of Ponzi Schemes Goes Deeper Than the Man Who Gave Them His Name.* [Online]. Available at: https://time.com/5877434/first-ponzi-scheme/ [Accessed 11 September 2020].

Weisul, 2018. *When It Comes to Revenue, Women Entrepreneurs Are Pummeling.* [Online]. Available at: https://www.inc.com/kimberly-weisul/boston-consulting-group-female-founders-higher-revenues.html [Accessed 11 October 2020].

West C., & Zimmerman D. H., 1987. Doing Gender. *Gender & Society.* 1987;1(2):125–51.

Which, 2020. *Pension calculator – How much will I have?*. [Online]. Available at: https://www.which.co.uk/money/pensions-and-retirement/options-for-cashing-in-your-pensions/overview-of-options-for-cashing-in-your-pension/pension-calculator-how-much-money-youll-have-a1jxm4d809k8 [Accessed 29 January 2021].

Wikipedia, 2021a. *Barings Bank*. [Online]. Available at: https://en.wikipedia.org/wiki/Barings_Bank [Accessed 14 March 2021].

Wikipedia, 2021b. *Deena Mehta*. [Online]. Available at: https://en.wikipedia.org/wiki/Deena_Mehta [Accessed 16 February 2021].

Windsor, L. C. et al., 2020. Gender in the time of COVID-19: Evaluating national leadership and COVID-19 fatalities. *Plos One*, 15(12).

Winnicott, D. W., 1956. Primary maternal preoccupation. In: *The Maturational Processes and the Facilitating Environment*. New York: International Universities Press. pp. 300–5.

Wittenberg-Cox, A., 2019. *France's Gender Balance Paradox*. [Online]. Available at: https://www.forbes.com/sites/avivahwittenbergcox/2019/05/20/frances-gender-balance-paradox/?sh=58d9326515ac [Accessed 11 November 2020].

Woolley, A. & Malone, T. W., 2011. *Defend Your Research: What Makes a Team Smarter? More Women*. [Online]. Available at: https://hbr.org/2011/06/defend-your-research-what-makes-a-team-smarter-more-women [Accessed 05 November 2020].

World Bank Blogs, 2018. *The gender gap in financial inclusion won't budge. Here are three ways to shrink it.* [Online]. Available at: https://blogs.worldbank.org/voices/gender-gap-financial-inclusion-three-ways-shrink-it [Accessed 10 October 2020].

World Health Organization, 2019. *Delivered by women, led by men: A gender and equity analysis of the global health and social workforce.* [Online]. Available at: https://apps.who.int/iris/handle/10665/311322 [Accessed 27 September 2020].

World Health Organization, 2021. *Gender and Genetics*. [Online]. Available at: https://www.who.int/genomics/gender/en/ [Accessed 13 April 2021].

Yellen, J. L., 2020. *The history of women's work and wages and how it has created success for us all.* [Online]. Available at: https://www.brookings.edu/essay/the-history-of-womens-work-and-wages-and-how-it-has-created-success-for-us-all/ [Accessed 17 July 2020].

Zenger, J., 2018. *The Confidence Gap in Men and Women: Why It Matters and How to Overcome It.* [Online]. Available at: https://www.forbes.com/sites/jackzenger/2018/04/08/the-confidence-gap-in-men-and-women-why-it-matters-and-how-to-overcome-it/?sh=26b432ed3bfa [Accessed 11 November 2020].

Zenger, J. & Folkman, J., 2019. *Research: Women Score Higher Than Men in Most Leadership Skills.* [Online]. Available at: https://hbr.org/2019/06/research-women-score-higher-than-men-in-most-leadership-skills [Accessed 17 November 2020].

Zimmermann, K. A., 2017. *History of Computers: A Brief Timeline.* [Online]. Available at: https://www.livescience.com/20718-computer-history.html [Accessed 29 November 2020].

INDEX